Y0-CQK-062

The Complete Book of Finches

by

Dr. Matthew M. Vriends

First Edition — First Printing

1987

HOWELL
BOOK HOUSE INC.
230 Park Avenue
New York, N.Y. 10169

Library of Congress Cataloging-in-Publication Data

Vriends, Matthew M., 1937-
  The complete book of finches.

  Bibliography: p. 203
  1. Finches. I. Title.
SF473.F5V75 1987   636.6'862   87-3960
ISBN 0-87605-825-X

The majority of the line illustrations appearing in this book were furnished by *E.P.J. Meijer* (The Netherlands).

Copyright © 1987 by Howell Book House Inc.

No part of this book may be used or reproduced in any manner whatsoever without written permission from the publisher, except in the case of brief excerpts quoted in reviews.

Printed in U.S.A.

THE COMPLETE BOOK OF FINCHES

**Other Fine Howell Books for the
Bird Owner's Library**

All About The Parrots, *Arthur Freud*
Bird Owner's Home Health and Care Handbook,
Gary A. Gallerstein, D.V.M.
Birds—A Guide to a Mixed Collection, *Irene Christie*
Breeding Cage and Aviary Birds, *Matthew M. Vriends*
The Complete Book of Canaries, *G.T. Dodwell*
The Complete Budgerigar, *Matthew M. Vriends*
The Complete Cockatiel, *Matthew M. Vriends*
Popular Parrots, *Matthew M. Vriends*

Uraeginthus bengalus

For Lucia and Tanya, with love

Soyons fidèles à nos faiblesses

Of course, animals do not really associate bars with prisons and they are quite happy as long as there is something nice to walk or climb on, for they do not really notice that the environment is artificial. There is of course, the well-known line. . . "A robin redbreast in a cage sets all heaven in a rage;" but robins live longer in cages than they do anywhere else and they are probably perfectly happy.

Sir Peter Scott
(in Martin, R. (ed.), *Breeding
Endangered Species in Captivity,*
Academic Press, London, 1975.)

Contents

About the Author

FOR MATTHEW M. VRIENDS, an abiding interest in the animal kingdom is a family affair that spans the generations.

A native of Eindhoven in the southern Netherlands, Dr. Vriends was strongly influenced by his father's example and involvement in the sciences. The elder Vriends was a celebrated writer and respected biology teacher. An uncle also loomed large in the Dutch scientific community, and the Natural History Museum at Asten, which annually welcomes over 200,000 visitors, is named in his honor.

Dr. Vriends vividly remembers the field trips he shared with both father and uncle and the "mini menagerie" maintained in the Vriends family home. The facilities for keeping and observing flora and fauna included a pair of large aviaries housing over 50 tropical bird species. A source of particular pride is the fact that many first breeding results came about in the Vriends family aviary.

Dr. Vriends' first published material appeared in magazines while he was still in high school. He wrote and illustrated his first bird book at 17—an amazing achievement that got young Vriends officially named the youngest biologist with a published work to his credit. This book was also an unqualified success with more than six reprints and sales in excess of 40,000 copies!

During his university career, Matthew Vriends continued to publish literary essays, poetry, short stories, a number of fine bird books and even a novel that helped finance his education.

After graduation he worked as a high school teacher, but eventually left education to devote more time to the serious study of ornithology. His work took him to some of the world's most exotic ports of call in Africa, South

Dr. Matthew M. Vriends

Lucy Vriends-Parent

America, Indonesia and Australia. And it was in Australia—home of many of the world's most beautiful and unusual bird species—that Matthew Vriends became fascinated with native parrots, parakeets and grassfinches. He remained in Australia from 1964 through 1967, absorbed in study and continuous publication of ornithological subjects.

A number of the books published during these years came to the attention of Prof. E.G. Franz Sauer, world-famous ornithologist, who succeeded in persuading Dr. Vriends to come to the University of Florida at Gainesville. Here Vriends worked with world-renowned biologists and to broaden his horizons, worked at the veterinary science and medical laboratories. One credit of which the author is particularly proud is having been allowed to work on the influenza virus research being conducted at that time.

Matthew Vriends earned his American doctorate in 1972, with a thesis on the Australian Masked Grassfinch (*Poephila personata*), and returned to Holland following the completion of his studies. Some time later he crossed the ocean again to take a position as the senior ornithology editor with a large American publishing firm until family concerns necessitated yet another return to the Netherlands in 1980. Vriends remained based in Holland until mid-1983, where he worked as an educator with additional interests in publishing and writing. He and his family now make their home outside Cincinnati, Ohio.

He remains an avid world-traveler, and, with his author-wife Lucy and daughter Tanya, regularly visits various countries of the world to observe the local wildlife close-up. His extensive travel also included an annual journey to the United States, where he is as well known and respected by the American avicultural community as by the Dutch.

As his father did, Matthew Vriends maintains a large, varied collection of animals in his home for both enjoyment and study. Fish, hamsters, gerbils, mice, rats, guinea pigs, turtles, dogs and, of course, birds—some 80 different species—constitute the current Vriends family menagerie. Happily, it appears that Tanya Vriends will be the third generation biologist/aviculturist in the family as she joins her parents with great enthusiasm in their interest.

Dr. Vriends generously shares his expertise in various ways. A popular international judge, he frequently officiates at bird shows in many countries. In Holland he was the host of a weekly radio program and conducted seminars on birds and other animals in conjunction with trade show appearances. His greatest fame has come through his writing and the helpful information he has imparted to pet owners and fanciers far and wide.

Currently Dr. Vriends is the author of some 80 books, in three languages, on birds, mammals, bees, turtles and fish, and over 1000 articles that have appeared in American and European magazines.

This remarkably prolific individual also enjoys music, painting, sketching, photography, tennis and gardening during rare moments of leisure when his attention is not directed to the natural sciences.

Dr. Matthew M. Vriends' accomplishments are like those of few others. By his varied activities in his chosen field, he has enlarged the body of knowledge for scientists, naturalists, diverse fancier groups and pet lovers around the world. His international reputation is earned through more than thirty years of education, achievement and enthusiastic devotion to science and aviculture.

THE PUBLISHER

Foreword

IN THIS BOOK, you will find a detailed description of some of the most colorful and popular cage and aviary birds from the tropics and subtropics: Waxbills, Mannikins, Munias, Grass and Parrot Finches, together forming the Family of Estrildid Finches or Estrildines (*Estrildidae*). Many of these cage and aviary birds can be procured in the pet trade.

Market channels for these birds are changing, however. Increasingly, their countries of origin are realizing the economic potential of their wildlife. Deforestation, however, is rapidly destroying wildlife habitats. Says the Pet Industry Joint Advisory Council (PIJAC): "Documentary evidence supports rates of deforestation between 50 and 75 acres per minute and upwards of 50,000 square miles per year because of agricultural and industrial expansion. Countries primarily affected are in the so-called Third World/underdeveloped areas such as Brazil (20% of rainforest destroyed by commercial cutting and mining); Indonesia (66 million acres classified as "denuded" by uncontrolled commercial cutting); Africa (1 million square kilometers of forest have been eliminated); Mexico (deforestation rate at 40,000 hectares/year), and Central America (almost two-thirds of Central America's lowland and lower mountain rain forest have been cleared or severely degraded since 1950)."

It is frightening to know that ". . . the world's rain forests will disappear altogether in 85 years if the present rate of 43,000 square miles per year continues," according to the Animal Welfare Institute.

Many countries, however, *are* improving their wildlife resource management, strengthening provisions of existing wildlife laws, and enforcing laws to protect endangered species. I fully applaud this development.

The result is that in the near future, the importation of many animals, including Estrildid Finches, will be cut off.

Bird fanciers have been accused for hundreds of years of posing a threat to the world's wild stock of birds. Of course, that's not true! In fact, thanks to aviculture, many, many bird species have been saved from total destruction. Many organizations are working to improve the process of importing birds. They are also making a more careful study of the medical aspects involved, to preclude danger of infection from imported birds for man and animals.

The plain and painful truth is that thousands upon thousands of birds are being slaughtered in their homelands every day. Mr. Marshall Meyers, general counsel of PIJAC, rightly says: "Indiscriminate killing for food, feathers or pest control does not serve conservation or mandate humane care. Throughout South America, Asia and Australia, numerous species are slaughtered (poisoned or shot) as agricultural pests. Many species are dislocated due to habitat destruction caused by agricultural and industrial expansion."

Years ago, as a high school student, I became serious about *raising* "simple" tropical finches and other birds. Many people who noticed how I went about it called me a fanatic, or worse. Why should I be so intent about feeding, housing, next boxes, temperature and humidity on behalf of birds that could be replaced at any pet store for a couple of quarters? They thought it even stranger when they found out that I made detailed observations about my breeding efforts and published the results in various bird journals.

Nowadays, however, the average bird fancier as well as the bird expert have clearly come to a different conclusion. Every right-minded bird fancier tries to expand the pet bird stock of our country, so that domestic breeding has completely (or almost completely) eliminated our dependence on imports. Many pet bird species, including many Estrildid Finches, have been domesticated, and imports of these species are no longer necessary. It is time to roll up our sleeves and develop effective programs to propagate other species in cages and aviaries before it is too late! The time will come when the breeding stock needed for such propagation will no longer be available because the birds may no longer be imported.

It is—I hope!—not too late, yet! It is well that I conducted those experiments with "plain, cheap birds" years ago, strange as my activities were regarded then. Let us work together to prevent the depredation of nature, so that it will remain dynamic in our time and that of our descendants.

I hope this book will contribute to this effort. Readers' comments or suggestions to improve the text or expand it will be gratefully received, and I will consider using them for any later printing of this book.

MATTHEW M. VRIENDS

Acknowledgements

I AM VERY GRATEFUL to the many aviculturists, curators of zoological societies and finch enthusiasts who have so generously helped me with this book. Particularly, thanks are due to those who have so kindly allowed me to use many of their notes on feeding, breeding, care and management of the Estrildid Finches (*Estrildidae*).

My grateful thanks are also due to biologist and countryman Mr. Max B. Heppner, M.Sc., of Baltimore, Maryland, for his friendship and his invaluable assistance in the preparation of this book.

Further I wish to thank Mr. R. Ceuleers and Mrs. P. Leijsen, of Herentals, Antwerp, Belgium; Mr. P. Kwast of Balk (Fr.), Holland, and last but not least my dear friend E. P. J. Meijer of Alphen (N.Br.), Holland, an excellent writer, artist and aviculturist, for his fine art work. Thanks a lot, Ed! This book could not have been produced without the help of these and other wonderful people!

Once again, I wish to thank my dear wife, Mrs. Lucia Vriends-Parent, and my charming daughter Tanya, for their constant encouragement and enthusiasm as well as their spontaneous cooperation in the preparation and actual writing of this book. Without their expertise and help this work could never have been completed.

All the opinions and conclusions expressed in the following pages are my own, however, and any errors must be my own responsibility.

M.M.V.

The handsome Gouldian Finch (*Chloebia gouldiae*) is one of the most popular finch species in aviculture. Shown here is a black-masked cock.

1

Estrildid Finches in Nature

Their Place in the Bird World

IN THE LAST 30 YEARS, many ornithologists have busied themselves intensively with the nomenclature of Waxbills, Mannikins, Munias and their allied species, the family *Estrildidae*. They have tried to specify exactly where in the world of birds these interesting and colorful species belong. I am not planning to go into extensive detail about this rather complicated topic in this book but I will make some reference to it without making any claims for thoroughness.

The family *Estrildidae* belongs to the suborder of songbirds (*Oscines*) which in turn belongs to the very extensive Order of *Passeriformes* (perching birds). At one time, Waxbills were known as Weaver Finches, because they had several traits in common with the true weavers (family *Ploceidae*). Thorough research has shown, however, that the Estrildine family possesses some characteristics that diverge from those of the Weavers. Body build (e.g. the structure of the syrinx or vocal organ), behavior (especially in association with nest building and incubation; various Weaver species have several hens simultaneously and are thus polygamous), and relationship to other birds all had an influence in justifying the change in nomenclature. The reclassification was also influenced by many important differences in anatomy, feather sketches, and most particularly ecological considerations of the relationship between organisms and their environment. The change in nomenclature is logical, actually, especially if we concentrate on nest building. The males of the true weavers (*Ploceidae*) begin by weaving a few blades or stems of grass around a twig. Only then do they form a ring-shaped construction to serve as a

17

side wall. When they have completed that part, they start building the roof, and only when the outside is completely finished do they commence paying attention to readying the inside of the nest. Weaver males build several nests before they begin their courtship song; they show their skills to their hens, which in turn pick one nest to raise a family.

The Estrildine family (*Estrildidae*) goes about nest building in a completely different manner. First they build a dish-shaped construction in a tree fork, and then they follow with the sides and roof. They never truly weave. That's why the name Weaver Finches is confusing, and it is better to classify them with the Grass and Parrot Finches (*Erythrurini*). This is most particularly true for the Australian Grass Finches, and for the Waxbills (*Esstrildini*), and Mannikins and Munias (*Amadini*).

Once this new classification was arrived at, you could also reclassify the Waxbills and their relatives, and so arrive at 34 genera that together have about 125 species. Regularly, new species or subspecies are being added, partially because almost every few years new species are being discovered and partially because species from other families are transferred to the ranks of the *Estrildidae*. Naturally, this results in continuous changes in the scientific names. Let me illustrate this with a specific example.

In all Australia, there is a single Zebra Finch species. Nonetheless, a number of ornithologists have thought to discover substantial color variants in certain areas. So, to make things more difficult, they recognized subspecies within this species. The old literature sometimes refers to three or more (up to seven) subspecies: *castanotis* (1837), *alexandrae* (1912), *hartogi* (1920), *mouki* (1912), *mungi* (1912), *roebucki* (1913) and *wayensis* (1912). In fact, these are all taxonomically identical to *castanotis,* although there are color variants in certain areas. J.A. Keast, an Australian ornithologist, however, proved irrefutably that there are no subspecies of Zebra Finches in Australia, as unlikely as this may seem, seeing the large territory on which Zebra Finches are found. Lack of subspecies in such a large territory is all the more unusual because the large annual drought in Central Australia forces the birds to move to areas with more water sources, which normally causes an intermixing with birds from other areas.

A modern bird book now almost consistently lists the classification of the Zebra Finch as *Taeniopygia* (or *Poephila*) *guttata.* This doesn't mean that individual finches from Australia can't differ in size, beak color and breast markings. And a truly different and officially recognized separate subspecies exists in fact on Timor and some other small Indonesian islands. The color of this Zebra Finch is brownish-yellow and the upper and back sides of the head are darker than in the Australian species. The females of the Timor species are darker on the back and breast than the Australian species. Still, the late ornithologist, Jean Delacour, maintained that all Zebra Finches, including the Indonesian variety, are one and the same. But this view is now regarded as mistaken.

18

Tri-colored or Blue-faced Parrot Finch (*Erythrua trichroa*).
Photo by author

Java Sparrow.   *Photo by Horst Müller*

International agreement on nomenclature has its purpose and function. The names often identify traits and characteristics of animals and plants: "*taeniopygia,* "a combination of two Greek words, for example, means "a tail with bands" (*tainia* = "band"; *pyge* = "rump, tail"); in Latin the word *gutta* means "drop" (*guttata* = "with drops"). *Poephila,* a Greek word, means "lover of grass" (*poë* = "grass"; *philos* = "to love"). The Greek word *castanotis* is a combination of two words: *castanon* = "chestnut", and *otos* (genitive of *ous*) = "ear." No wonder the Zebra Finch is sometimes called Chestnut-eared Finch!

Conversely, the nonscientific nomenclature, whether in, for example, English, French, German, or Dutch, is often a thorn in the side of many biologists. Often, a single animal or plant is called by several different names that are frequently recognized only locally. And often the same name is given to quite different species! It's impossible to sort out. That is why I recommend that you remember the scientific name of birds that interest you, even if the above discussion gives you the chills. Granted, it isn't easy, and I don't make the whole thing any more attractive by pointing out that the classification I use in this book may not hold forever in the future. But you can worry about that when the time comes!

Country of Origin and Its Climate

The *Estrildidae* came from the Old World; the majority of the species originated in Africa some 30 million years ago (the end of the Miocene period). Most representatives can still be found in Africa, south of the Sahara, and Malagasy (formerly Madagascar). They can also be found in southern Asia (up to Taiwan) and in Australia, but not in New Zealand. In Australia there are 18 "native" Grass Finches and one imported one, the Spice Finch (*Lonchura punctulata*). Australian Grass Finches closely resemble True Finches (*Fringillidae*), Weavers and Sparrows, but can be distinguished by the presence of 10 primary wing feathers rather than the nine found in the True Finches. We can also find *Estrildidae* in New Guinea, Indonesia, the Philippines, and many islands of the western Pacific. Naturally, people have moved various species of birds from one area to another over the centuries. Some adapted marvelously, like the previously cited Spice Finch, for example. Often they even displaced the original species, but more often they died out in time.

Finches inhabit various habitats, but their favorite is open country. They are also found along the margins of forests, in forested flat lands and not too dense forests. Generally, they have water in the immediate neighborhood (brook, river or lake), and in the tall growth at the water's edge they often like to build their nest.

Many species follow man into his habitation, and you can find nests in fields, parks, and gardens, and even under roofs, in rain pipes and other "unnatural" locations. Working in Australia, my wife and I encountered Grass Finches in the strangest places. We found Bicheno's Finches (*Stizoptera*

[*Poephila*] *bichenovii*) close to a wasp nest; Black-throated Finches (*Poephila cincta*) in the bottom of the nest of birds of prey; Sydney Waxbills (*Aegintha temporalis*) in the rose bushes of a city garden; and Spice Finches (*Lonchura punctulata*) in a fissure of an old garden shed. Many Fire Finches (*Lagonosticta* spp.) live close to people, and you can often find their nests under roofs, in the holes of telephone poles, and such. You can even find Rice Finches (*Padda oryzivora*), from Asia, in stables and barns.

Estrildidae are true children of the sun, since they come from tropical and subtropical climates originally. Even after several generations of domestic breeding, they are still extremely sensitive to temperature changes. Recently imported birds, therefore, must be gradually acclimatized (see page 36).

The temperatures of the country of origin are totally different (or nearly so) from the temperatures in the United States. I will go into more detail later, but let me say here that in many states—those with cold and humid autumns and winters—you can't expect to keep *Estrildidae* all year in an outdoor or garden aviary. In early fall, they must be moved indoors and kept in a warm place at room temperature. Research has indicated that tropical finches really feel comfortable at temperatures between 65° and 90° F (18° and 32° C). The upper limit of this range is not essential for all species; you can look up the details under the individual descriptions of the various species. Still, in my experience, birds I have raised felt most at ease and comfortable inside that range, even when they were aviary bred.

There are some species, the Gouldian Finch (*Chloebia gouldiae*), for example, that won't breed successfully in their country of origin unless the temperature reaches about 104° F (40° C). Gouldian Finches live primarily in the Kimberley District of Australia, where the temperature ranges from 107° to 122° F (42° to 50° C). If temperatures fall below 86° F (30° C), the birds continue to flourish, but not as actively as with a higher temperature. They become sluggish and droopy with temperatures under 60° F (15° C), which can be noticed clearly even in wild birds during the rainy season. In the wild, they won't attempt to breed when temperatures fall below about 73° F (23° C).

Most bird breeders in Europe and America, therefore, keep their birds in cages and aviaries located in attics, dens, enclosed porches, and garages, where temperatures can be controlled. When birds are recently imported, the new arrivals are always kept indoors in a temperature of at least 85° F (30° C). With temperatures that high, you should not forget to furnish several dishes of water or several humidifiers to keep up the humidity that is essential for a proper environment. It is important to maintain a constant temperature and humidity in places where birds are bred or quarantined. The humidity in a room with 75° F (25° C) should remain between 65 and 70 percent.

There are *Estrildidae*-species that are less sensitive in this respect than others but none can tolerate large temperature changes. If you live in an area where the nights are cold and especially humid, you must provide proper

21

shelter in the outdoor aviary by means of a night shelter, a generous supply of nest boxes (that can be used for sleeping), or dense bushes. Birds originating from wooded regions can't withstand changes in temperatures and humidity as well as birds from open country, where nights can be intensely cold— sometimes down to freezing temperatures. So listen to the weather forecast for predictions that can cause problems for your stock, and then take the proper precautions.

Food Sources in the Wild

You can tell by their keg-shaped beaks that Estrildines are principally seed eaters. This fact shouldn't be taken literally by those of us who maintain birds in captivity. You can't just expect to maintain them with a cup of some kind of seed mix. To keep them in good condition, you must supplement the seeds with universal food, egg food, "ant eggs," chopped mealworms, and fruit (apple, pear, berry, banana, orange, date, soaked raisin), and green food (lettuce, chickweed, endive, and sprouted seed) as well as cuttle bone. We'll discuss this topic in more detail later; at this point, I merely want to emphasize that feeding only a tropical seed mix is no guarantee that our ornamental finches are properly nourished.

A closer look at the bills of the various types of Estrildines shows that some of them have a strong, keg-shaped beak; we call them Waxbills. Others have a beak that is much lighter in construction; we call those Grass Finches. There are others, as well.

Even in the wild, finches do not live on seed alone. Especially in the breeding season, the birds look industriously for spiders, flies, mosquitoes, small bugs, termites and such. Therefore, although it is illegal in the United States, European fanciers release Tiger Finches, also called Strawberry Finches or Red Avadavat (*Amandava amandava*), during the breeding season, so that they can busily look for all types of insects in the yard. They love it. They must be full-time inhabitants of a garden aviary and completely accustomed to living there. They don't start until the female has laid her first egg, and then, they don't bother them. Furthermore, they don't reduce the quality and quantity of the food provided. They don't want to cause the birds to "worry" about getting a full meal for themselves or their young. Finally, the risk of an experiment like this is considerable; the birds may fly off into the wild blue yonder!

Wild Estrildines look principally for ripe and near-ripe grass and weed seed. They particularly like various grass and grain species. It is a special sight to watch the colorful birds maneuver around the seedhead of a long-stemmed grain to pick at the seeds. It isn't hard to observe this behavior in the flatland species. Wild birds also like reed seed as well as flower and leaf buds, berries, young greens, and naturally sprouting grass and weed seeds; during the breeding season they prefer spiders and insects, especially when feeding their young.

22

Birds that live in the woods and along rivers and streams have a rich variety and quantity of seed available almost throughout the entire year. Those living on the flat lands annually experience recurring periods of drought and thus have to make do with dry types of seed. Many large flocks move to the coast or elsewhere to look for food, especially many Australian finches. You can find the birds in large numbers at the strangest places, as long as there is a bountiful supply of food. Species known to be nonmigratory can go on the move during certain years when necessity forces them into moving hundreds of miles in search of sustenance. There is nothing abnormal about this. And in addition to lack of food, a shortage of water is reason enough to move on.

In the rainy season, of course, the birds don't lack for food and water. Barren regions transform into beautiful green habitats, where the birds have everything to their liking. They can find a good supply of their favorite insects. Flying termites and mosquitoes especially are caught and eaten by the thousands every day! This emphasizes that birds known as true seedeaters depend on insects as an important source of nourishment, especially because insects are used as food for the young in the nest. The parent birds generally strip branches and stems to find the insects, in addition to catching insects in flight or on the ground.

There are exceptions, however. We know of several finch species that won't have anything to do with insects. This is most particularly true of the Pintailed Nonpareil (*Erythrura prasina*) of Indonesia and nearby regions, a totally seed-eating species. Even the young are raised entirely as vegetarians. At the other end of the scale is the Orange-winged Pytilia (*Pytilia afra*) from East Africa, which is an exceptional insect-eater even outside of the breeding season.

I could go on with more examples, but the birds themselves will show you where their preferences lie. Those with a pointed beak are, in addition to being seed-eaters, also lovers of insects and small spiders, which they also offer to their young. Those with a more keg-shaped beak can be generally regarded as *primarily* seed-eaters.

Some finches drink their water in a way that differs from the scooping motion commonly seen in chickens and other birds. These birds can take in water in a continuous sucking motion; among them are many Australian finches, including the Diamond Finch (*Stagonoplura guttata*), the Zebra Finch (*Taeniopygia* [*Poephila*] *guttata*), the Owl Finch or Double-barred Finch (*Stizoptera* [*Poephila*] *bichenovii*), the Gouldian Finch (*Chloebia gouldiae*), the Long-tailed Finch (*Poephila acuticauda*), and the Black-throated or Parson Finch (*Poephila cincta*).

The Breeding Season

Breeding is a natural instinct to maintain the species. When this instinct

23

manifests itself, the breeding season begins. Generally, this occurs in spring, but there are birds that start earlier or later.

Internally, the birds start this process with what can best be described as "a fever," in the good sense of the word. The internal temperature rises, not throughout the whole body but just in the areas where it is necessary, in the so-called brood spots, which are pressed against the eggs during brooding. Brood spots, areas where a large supply of blood is found, differ sharply in various species. The way eggs are "set on" is determined, among other factors, by the shape of the nest, the location of the brood spots and their size and intensity, and the size of the clutch of eggs. Just look at the difference between a Zebra Finch (*Taeniopygia* [*Poephila*] *guttata*) and a water bird, and you will immediately understand.

As indicated earlier, availability of appropriate food is a determining factor whether wild birds will start breeding. Species living on the flat lands will need to have insects available to feed their young in addition to seeds. This food is available only when there is adequate precipitation. Rain promotes plant growth so that birds have available fresh grass stems, moss, plant down and other necessary nesting materials. If conditions are favorable in nature and the rains bring adequate vegetation, you can notice that in a short period of time the birds will raise two or even three broods, one after the other. You can tell that the birds are "in a hurry" by noticing that a female is brooding eggs while the young of the previous brood are still in the nest, now under the exclusive care of the male. Gouldian Finches (*Chloebia gouldiae*) even have the young of earlier broods help feed their brothers and sisters of a succeeding brood.

During the breeding season, large flocks of ornamental finches often separate to have plenty of food and nesting material available to all, even though most species don't break off the colony or group bond. It's a fact that Estrildid Finches love company and therefore stay in groups and share feast and famine together. You can still observe this in the breeding season. They make nests in close proximity, sometimes even in the same tree or bush. This is a characteristic trait of *Estrildidae*, which differentiates them from the True Finches (*Fringillidae*), where each pair sets up its own territory that is defended against any undesirable intruder, including members of their own species. One of the *Estrildidae*, the Crimson Finch (*Neochmia phaeton*), a rarely available species, is an exception, however. These birds are extremely territorial and chase out small and large birds, including members of their species.

The social behavior of the Estrildid Finches can be noted clearly among Zebra Finches (*Taeniopygia* [*Poephila*] *guttata*). These well-known birds conduct special meetings during the day in the breeding season, social hours in which they appear to discuss the events of the day with other Zebra Finches, while preening each other's feathers.

During the breeding season, the male goes in search of a mate, although

24

the female determines the final choice of a partner. The search for a mate is called the mating dance. This dance is accompanied by song or the exhibition of certain, often colorful parts of the plumage. Almost all the Grass Finches hold a blade of grass, a piece of straw, or a feather in the beak while performing the mating dance.

Once mates are selected, the newly formed couples go off and spend much time close together; especially in the early afternoon, they preen each other's feathers, or just sit pressed together on a branch, smooching while they sun themselves. It is known that the majority of the *Estrildidae* in the wild, form pairs that remain together for life. By the way, there are some finches that don't engage in any particular physical contact, such as preening; the Gouldian Finch (*Chloebia gouldiae*), for example, never, or hardly ever engages in bodily contact.

When the female is ready to breed, you can see this clearly by her behavior. She presses herself down against a branch and quiveringly beats her tail in an up-and-down motion. In some species, the female also utters a few notes of song with her head held high, or she holds a long blade of grass, a feather, or a thin twig in the beak. (This occurs, for example, in Cordon-bleus and their relatives—*Uraeginthus spp.*) During mating, and frequently also before, the female utters short, trilling sounds. It is consistently the female that invites the male to copulate. Mating can occur several times in succession.

After mating, the heavy work begins. The male will look for a suitable spot to build a nest, and the female will inspect what he finds. She is definitely choosy and may reject ten or more locations. Once she accepts a choice, the male goes in search of building material. The female usually takes the role of architect. Most nests are bullet or bottle shaped and are covered by a roof. Most nests also have a small tunnel as entrance. Usually, nests are built in the open in thorny bushes, trees, or grass stems. There are species that use tree hollows or abandoned nests of weavers and other birds. These adopted nests are almost always restored and reconstructed before re-use.

Favored construction material includes fresh and dried blades of grass, moss, wool, plant fibers and down, twigs, and small branches. To line the nest, small feathers, plant down, soft grass, hair, wool, and moss are put to use.

The size and shape of nests built by the various species vary sharply. Most nests, however, are rather small, seven inches (18 cm.) or less in diameter, down to three inches (7 or 8 cm.). I do know of nests, however, with a diameter of eight to ten inches (20 to 25 cm.).

Prof. Dr. Karl Immelmann has estimated that it takes between 1,800 and 2,000 separate blades of grass (the principal construction material) to build a nest. Some ornamental finches have very specific nest sites, as, for example, in the neighborhood of wasp nests or the eyries of birds of prey (like the Diamond Finch—*Stagonopleura guttata*). Still other species move into abandoned nest tunnels in the banks of waterways or in holes drilled into trees by woodpeckers and other birds. There are even species that build nests in termite hills.

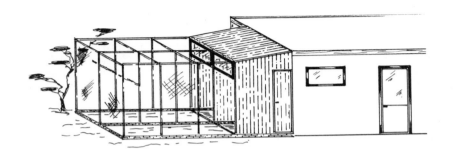

A practical design for a finch aviary.

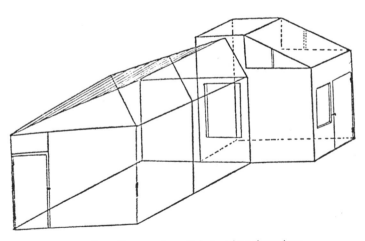

Schematic diagram of a well-designed garden aviary.

The height at which Estrildines build nests is also characteristic. The large majority builds low, or even at ground level. We may take it as a general rule that nests will rarely be more than thirteen feet (4 meters) off the ground. Only those species that increasingly move into human settlements are likely to build considerably higher. Zebra Finches (*Taeniopygia* [*Poephila*] *guttata*), Spice Finches (*Lonchura punctulata*) and Star Finches (*Neochmia* [*Bathila*] *ruficauda*) are good examples of this. Species that build very close to the ground include the Nuns or Munias (*Lonchura spp.*) and the Cordon-bleus (*Uraeginthus spp.*); one that builds right on the ground is the Common, or Black-chinned Quail Finch (*Ortygospiza atricollis*).

Usually, nest construction takes several days, although there are species that take somewhat longer. The job doesn't have to be lengthy because the usual nest is quite small. Actually, the process is rather slow. The birds add just a bit of building material to the nest in any one day, and they continue the process while the nest is in use. While they take turns brooding and looking for food, the two parents often bring along additional building material. They use the item to wave to one another and then work it into the nest, seemingly as a pastime. There are even finches that build nests outside the breeding season, but generally these nests aren't built as tightly and are used only to spend the night. Some also build sleeping nests during the breeding period for use by the young that have left the regular nest.

The eggs are generally pure white and are laid in clutches of four to six.

Usually, both parents take turns brooding during the day, but at night they set on the nest together. It can happen that the female broods alone during the night, while the male keeps watch nearby. I discovered that the Masked Finch (*Poephila personata*) also takes turns at night even if both parent birds stay in the nest. Each parent spends a period of about two hours brooding.

Brooding by turns during the day can vary considerably in length. For example, Red-eared Waxbills (*Estrilda troglodytes*) take turns of approximately three hours, while other species brood one or two hours. Not all males are devoted participants, however, and leave most of the job to the female. The brooding period takes about 11 to 16 days depending on the weather, the breaks for socializing that many birds take during the early afternoon, the temperature and humidity, the time of year that breeding began, and the intensity of brooding. Actual brooding isn't begun until the third or fourth egg has been laid, which leads to the situation that the first eggs laid hatch with only a time differential of a few hours while the later eggs hatch two or three days after the others.

Newly hatched young are blind and naked, although they may have a little patch of down here and there. Therefore, the first week the hatchlings are kept warm with care. After a week, the little eyes open, and down starts to grow on their tail and wings. The smaller species of ornamental finches leave the nest between the age of 18 and 21 days; the larger ones, between 22 and 25 days.

As stated earlier, many species build special sleeping nests during the period that they are brooding, so that the young have a place to sleep once they are ready to leave the parental nest. Some birds, however, direct recent fledglings back to the parental nest for the first few nights.

When the young have been out of the parental nest for two or three weeks, they can be regarded as independent. At that point, they may start to make playful attempts at mating (even with young of the same sex), but they can't by any means actually copulate. They will exchange baby feathers for adult feathers at three months of age and then, generally, they can't be distinguished from the parent birds. Even the beak is in full color. (At hatch, the bill is ivory and later becomes a black horn color.)

Young birds' plumage is not as colorful as that of the parents. At first, they look greyish, greenish, or brownish, which is a good camouflage against the predacious eyes of birds and other hunting animals.

In general, all nestlings among the Estrildid Finches strongly resemble each other. Only the mouth, palate, inside of the lower mandible, and the tongue markings differ noticeably from species to species. The most noticeable markings consist of knobby papillae in the corners of the mouth, which can be blue, yellow or white. In addition, there are black round and oval patches on the palate, tongue and on the inside of the lower beak, as stated. These markings enable us to distinguish between the young of various species. The young of the Blue-faced Parrot Finch (*Erythrura trichroa*) have bright blue tubercles, without distinguishable markings on the tongue and palate. The Gouldian Finch (*Chloebia gouldiae*), however, has many markings on the tongue and palate. In short, the mouth markings of Estrildid nestlings are, as mentioned, characteristic for the species. Furthermore, not all Estrildines, the Orange-cheeked Waxbill (*Estrilda melanotis*), for example, have these markings.

Once the young are independent, the markings disappear, but there are species that do maintain them, although often in a somewhat less intense form. By the way, there is a kind of background pattern discernible in these markings. In general, the beak pattern consists of five black, round patches, which can be seen clearly because the palate is pale pink. On the tongue, two dark patches can be seen, and on the inside of the lower beak, there is a half round series of small patches. The beak papillae are often somewhat phosphorescent. The general purpose of the markings is to show the parent birds precisely where they should deposit the food they're carrying in. That's important, because the inside of the enclosed nest is almost completely dark. Furthermore, the markings stimulate the parents to bring in food, and they recognize their own young by the markings without error. I discovered this clearly when I once had to move some nestlings to a foster nest. The adoptive parents were of the same species and were good providers. The foster birds had somewhat deviant but very small markings. (Nature is not static, but dynamic and individual animals differ, just as human beings do.) Well, the

28

adoptive parents refused to feed the transferred babies! Let me add that this is unusual. Most parent birds accept foster babies from the same or closely related species.

The feathers of young birds that haven't molted have characteristic colors that differ among species. Often there is a lined or patchy design in yellow, white, red, or blue. In this connection, it is interesting to note that there are certain Whydahs that parasitize members of the families of *Estrilda, Pytilia, Uraeginthus* and *Lagonosticta*; the young of both species cannot be distinguished from one another, a fact to which we will return later.

Young birds being fed in the nest can assume several begging postures. Zebra Finches seem to be able to turn their head 180 degrees or lay it on the shoulder. Black-billed Magpies (also called Bronze-winged Mannikin or Hooded Finch) (*Lonchura* [*Spermestes*] *cucullatus*) beat their wings back and forth excitedly. Young of most species just move their raised head up and down in a rocking motion and utter an urgent begging cry; they don't move their wings, in contrast with the young of the True Finches (*Fringillidae*).

To feed the young, the parent bird regurgitates food with pumping motions into the throat of the nestlings, which close their beak on that of the feeding parent. If the young bird doesn't swallow the food quickly enough (the swallowing reflex), the parent retracts the bit of food and inserts it into another opened mouth. The young that swallows quickly has an empty crop and thus is hungry. This technique seems to work excellently and all young are fed on time (a parent bird would be hard put to remember which of the begging little ones should get the next turn).

In addition to providing food, the parents warm the young the first nine to twelve days, and, of course, also protect the young. After a couple of weeks, the young have grown so much that there isn't enough room inside the nest any more. Often the young birds are somewhat bigger than their parents at that point; after all, they are extremely well fed and barely use any energy. So then the parents no longer bring food inside the nest but feed them from the edge of the nest or from the entrance.

As fledglings, the young remain in close proximity to each other and continue to be fed principally by the male parent, on the ground or on a low branch or twig. You can often see them sitting neatly in a row, enjoying the tidbits they are fed. Meanwhile, the female has already started a new clutch in most cases.

Brooding Parasitism

I have made previous reference to the fact that a number of principally African Estrildid species are maneuvered into becoming foster parents by "brooding parasites," of which the Whydahs are the most well-known. These birds belong to a subfamily of the Weavers and thus are not related at all to the finches. Despite this, the true offspring in the nest can't be distinguished from the interlopers; they have identical mouth markings and later the same feather colors; they also have the same begging cries and begging positions. You can't tell them apart until they complete their first molt. Only when, as young males, they manifest their first bird song can you notice a difference between the two species, and that is true only for a rather limited number of species. The greater majority adopts the song of the foster parent, so that Whydahs sing like some of the Estrildids.

The majority of the Whydahs have species-specific foster parents. For example, the Paradise Whydah (*Vidua paradisa*) only goes for the nests of the Melba Finch (*Pytilia melba*), and the Broad-tailed Paradise Whydah (*Vidua orientalis obtusa*) for the Orange-winged Pytilia (*Pytilia afra*). Let me add that the eggs of the two parasitizing species also look identical in size and color (white) to those of the hosts. This opens up a whole new territory for the aviculturist—raising Whydahs with the aid of the appropriate foster parents. This, however, would require a quite roomy outdoor aviary.

Song

The song of Estrildids is generally quiet and unobtrusive, in contrast with the True Finches (*Fringillidae*), real song birds that include some exceptional performers. The ornamental finches, however, do have a sometimes rich variety of enticing and whistling calls, each of which have a definite meaning. You can distinguish warnings, begging, invitations for social contact, and others, which can be used alone or in combination.

Not all ornamental finches should be considered "unmusical." Quite well known is the varied song of the Dybowski Twin-spot (*Euschistospiza dybowskii*), a bird that somewhat resembles the Painted Finch (*Emblema picta*), and has drawn considerable interest in the last 20 years.

The song of many birds has a quite specific function, namely to establish boundaries for their territory and to warn away trespassers of their own species. The sound made by male Estrildids can be distinguished best when it is used as an enticing call during the mating dance, to invite mating, and to begin nest building. It also serves as a way for mates to maintain contact, as a social contact, as a warning, or as an invitation to form a flock.

It is interesting to note that the soft, hoarse song of the Spice Finch (*Lonchura punctulata*) or the "near" singing of the Gouldian Finch (*Chloebia gouldiae*) appears to be solidly appreciated by members of the species in the wild, even though it seems hard to hear much less to understand by the human ear. When these birds bring forth their "aria," other males, particularly young ones, group themselves around the "lead singer" to be able to learn to sing right, as it were. Females also appear to take lessons, but they can't learn to sing. Why they attend is anybody's guess, although listening to the different calls, they probably learn the meaning. Let me mention, however, that there are certain species of finches in which the females do learn a pretty good song, Cordon-bleus (*Uraeginthus spp.*), for example.

Life Expectancy

Research over the years has shown without doubt that the small species of birds seldom live more than three years *in the wild*. Many ornithologists say they only attain a maximum of two years. This is easy to believe when we realize that most birds are exposed to all types of dangers. In this connection, we should not forget the negative role played by mankind through the ages, and continuing today. Industrialization robs birds of entire habitats. To that, add water and air pollution, insecticides, noise, and other factors that have been amply discussed and written about. They all have a negative influence, not only on birds, but on all animals and plants, and reduce their life expectancy considerably. Natural causes can also do a great deal of damage to animals and plants; I'm thinking about heavy storms, tropical rain showers, hail, frost and the like. All this affects the ornamental finches—and other animals! In particular, the large-scale deforestation being carried out at the moment, which ruins the natural habitat of many species, is devastating. In addition, the tropics and subtropics are home to many natural enemies that live on birds and their eggs. The effect of predatory birds, mice, rats, snakes, and even insects like termites, should not be understated. And finally, parasites like coccidia, bacteria, worms, and such also see to it that the life span of wild birds remains quite limited.

It is very different in an aviary, where the birds get optimum care, feeding, and housing, and are protected from their enemies. In cold weather, they get heat; in sickness, they have access to our entire bird apothecary. Insecticides pose no threat, because their green food is carefully washed or even raised organically. So, it is no great surprise that finches in captivity live at least twice as long as those in the wild, so small finches that attain five to eight years are no exception. It is even possible to obtain good results when breeding with these "oldsters." The hardiest species can become 10 to 15 years old. My professional experience as a zoologist has convinced me that the bird fancy doesn't harm nature. Rather, the fancier with his heart in his hobby is much more likely to be an effective force to preserve what remains in nature, especially if he makes a *solid effort to breed the birds he is keeping!*

2

Housing, Management and Care

Adequate Housing

ADEQUATE HOUSING REPRESENTS a crucial part of what is needed for success in the bird fancy. A major reason is that good housing promotes proper environmental temperature, an important factor for breeding exotics, particularly finches.

Altogether, there are about 8,600 species of birds in the world, and during the millenia they have become adapted to the conditions under which they have to live and raise their young. One major environmental factor that has affected the development of birds is warmth, and adaptions were made to provide proper protection against bitter cold or extreme heat.

Penguins, for example, have a thick layer of fat that protects against cold and stores energy on which the birds can draw if it is necessary to survive without food. By contrast, the tender exotics that live in the tropics have little to protect themselves against cold, and they must take in food frequently to maintain their body temperature.

One of the reasons why some fanciers lose their small exotics in winter is that they don't sufficiently realize that at that time of year there are at least 14 hours of darkness and that during this time the birds can't eat. As a result, they don't maintain their body temperature. Their crops are empty in the morning, and the cause of their death is often starvation. The solution is to provide several hours of artificial light in the evening, remembering, however, that a bird needs 10 to 12 hours of darkness each day to ensure adequate rest.

It doesn't take any special gadgetry to supply exotics with the environmental temperature they need. If these birds are properly acclimatized, they can live and breed under any climatic condition. And I must add that although most birds can't stand being exposed to direct, bright sunlight, this doesn't mean that they can't withstand high temperatures. It is quite hot in the tropics, even in the shade of trees and shrubs. The heat is accompanied by a very dry atmosphere that can't be compared with the hot, humid weather we experience here during a heatwave. In most instances, reports of successful breeding of difficult birds indicate that the weather during the breeding season was exceptionally hot.

The body temperature of birds is about 10 degrees F. higher than that of humans. All in all, we must create a situation for exotics that parallels the hot, dry weather in their land of origin. Since in many areas we ordinarily don't experience hot spells that last more than a few weeks, we must find ways to create and maintain a high daytime temperature. Night temperature is not as important, since even in the tropics, this can fall quite a bit.

What's the best way to go about this?

One way is to set up a bird room with a thermostatically controlled heating system and electric ventilators, but the average breeder can't afford this level of luxury. The most available source of heat is the sun, and the facility for raising birds should be arranged so that maximum use is made of sunlight. The facility should not be too large, because a large volume of air is difficult to heat; also, heat is lost quickly if the surface area of the floor, walls, and ceiling is relatively large when compared to the volume of air they contain. A space of about 12′ × 9′ × 6′ is convenient and simple to heat. In a room this size, you can install a reasonable number of flight cages with access to outside areas.

The building should be oriented with the front facing south, so that sunshine can warm it as long as possible. The birds enjoy the sun also. It is amazing how much the indoor temperature can rise if exposed to even the relatively weak rays of winter sun. If you have a bird house that uses available sunlight effectively, you then need to find a method to retain heat when the sun doesn't shine. It is a matter of insulation. There are several types of insulation available on the market to put on the walls. Yet, a basic requirement is that there is enough space between the outside and inside wall to retain a proper amount of still air. Pay special attention to windows. They are good to have, but lose heat easily. Install double windows, with sufficient space between the storm windows and regular windows. A properly fitted door is also important for retaining heat and avoiding drafts.
and avoiding drafts.

A second important factor is proper ventilation. With higher temperatures, air turns stale quicker if there is no supply of fresh air. Air therefore needs to be circulated more frequently in summer than in winter, especially with an eye to retaining warmth in winter. The simplest method of ventilation is to have slots for air intake at the bottom on all four sides and with an exhaust slot in the roof, properly protected against rain. The slots should be closable with a slide, so that the airflow can be regulated. The slots open to the wind should be closed immediately and the others should be completely opened. The openings should be covered with fine mesh to keep vermin out.

To maintain proper heat and ventilation in winter is necessary if you want to maintain your birds in good condition and in good health. Heating should not be overdone. The major purpose of a high temperature is to stimulate birds to breed, and that, of course, is not useful in winter.

The best way to avoid problems with heat is to retain an inside temperature between 77° and 82° F (25° and 28° C), plus access to an open flight cage, so that the birds can choose for themselves. Even if there is much to attract the birds to the open flight cage, the higher temperature inside will draw them there when necessary.

High temperatures have some drawbacks, but these can be overcome. First, you need to guard against food spoilage, particularly egg food, nectar, and insects. Green food wilts fast and dries out, so provide these items in small quantities and replace them often.

Another factor is that water evaporates more rapidly. I have found that replacing water early in the morning and early in the evening is adequate. I also recommend automatic waterers, which actually lose very little water through evaporation. Another way to reduce evaporation is to buy chick waterers.

Birds will show you when they are sweltering by sitting with open beaks and drooping wings. (They don't have sweat glands in the skin, like humans.) If you see these signs, you must take steps immediately to lower the temperature. Actually, installing a reliable thermometer is better, though, for avoiding such stressful situations. Hang the thermometer at the height of the perches, because the temperature can vary considerably between the floor and the ceiling. Also, remember to disturb birds as little as possible when the temperature is high, because body movements cause body temperature to rise, which can have tragic results.

If you need to catch birds in warm weather, do this early in the morning, or at night, when it is cooler. Remember that heat dries out the air. Even though the humidity should be kept low for most finches, it pays to sprinkle water on the floor once or twice daily. Or you can place potted plants (safe varieties!) nearby and keep them moist to avoid having the air dry out.

Proper attention to environmental factors is extremely important, especially if you want to breed Estrildines. Observe and experiment with the birds you want to raise, and you will be able to breed a variety of species. I want to urge you to grow from a keeper to a breeder of birds. Unless you've experienced it, it's hard to imagine how fascinating it is to observe courtship

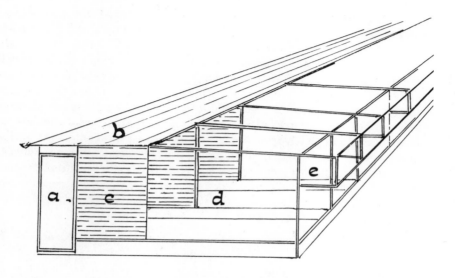

Diagram showing a multiple aviary unit with the following component parts: a) door to the night shelter; b) translucent or opaque panels providing light to the shelter; c) partitions for privacy; d) mesh; e) feeding area.

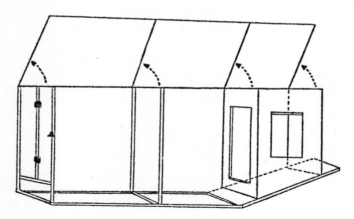

Another design for a garden aviary.

and nest building and how exciting to watch the laying of eggs, the feeding of young, and the busy activities of enthusiastic bird parents.

Keep good notes and records to supplement published information about your birds. You will find an extensive book list in the back of this volume to discover all you need to know.

Well prepared and equipped, you will be able to extend the fellowship of breeders that helps itself to a good supply of birds independent of imports, which are becoming more and more difficult to obtain. As pointed out earlier, there are all kinds of factors that threaten the supply of wild birds. Responsible breeding in captivity can help prevent certain bird species from disappearing completely from the face of the earth. For example, Australian Grass Finches are becoming increasingly popular, showing that the aviculturist can accomplish a great deal, when considering that imports have been cut off for many years!

Quarantining And Acclimatizing Imports

The cost of imported birds today is determined to a large degree by the cost of quarantine after arrival. Government officials deem it necessary that every bird entering the country must be placed into quarantine for at least 30 days, whether it is an exotic finch or a parrot. The major concern is exotic Newcastle Disease (VVND—Velogenic Viscerotropic Newcastle), a dreaded virus infection which several years ago caused major losses among chickens. There is no doubt that the poultry industry suffered millions of dollars in losses, so that it makes sense that the government releases imports into the domestic trade only after they have been medically examined and found to be free of this infection. Birds that die during quarantine are carefully examined and the cause of death is precisely determined. It is a system that works satisfactorily even though it raises opposition from time to time. There can be no doubt that it's important to bring only virus-free birds into the domestic trade channels. And yes, it is expensive, too, when you add all the direct and indirect costs involved, but much cheaper than acquiring an infected bird, then losing an entire collection.

Some hobbyists have been considering importing their own birds using a government operated quarantine station. This is no simple matter, however. In the first place, you need to know reliable sources overseas, and you must count on going through a lot of paperwork. Secondly, you need to realize that this approach is far from inexpensive. You need to count on paying a customs broker between $500 and $1,000 and maintenance costs per bird of approximately 60 cents per day. The entire quarantine of minimally 30 days thus costs at least $18 per bird. To that you must add the cost of purchase, transportation to the quarantine station and more transportation costs from there to your home. Don't be surprised if altogether a pair of exotic finches will cost you $80 or more. And remember that if one of your birds dies in quarantine, you have to stand the loss because the person operating the quarantine station is not responsible. You not only lose the bird itself but all the money you have previously spent on it. All in all, it is generally cheaper and safer to purchase birds from a breeder or a pet store.

Government regulations and requirements for imports are becoming more and more complex, so you need to count on domestic breeding. The supply of certain species is already limited, the birds have become expensive, and this is likely to worsen. Many species may become unattainable.

While on the subject of regulations, be aware that in many places you need a permit or license to keep birds. There are neighborhood covenants that flatly prohibit the keeping of any pet whatsoever. There are also localities that limit the number of birds that you may keep in a residential neighborhood. Still other locations require that you get an occupational license before you can sell birds, even if you raise them yourself. Further, local ordinances may require commercial zoning if you want to sell birds. Some places permit the sale of birds, but not any advertisement on your property that offers "Birds For Sale"; there, you have to place ads in the local newspaper. There are states requiring a state license to sell birds, even those you've raised yourself. Be aware of ordinances of this type. It may seem burdensome, but unless you stay informed you may get into trouble sooner or later, which can be quite costly. Make inquiries from the local government and join a local bird club. Your fellow members will certainly provide you with full details about what may and may not be done. If they can't do this (and this has occurred far too often!), insist that the leadership inform itself fully and immediately on any restrictions and licenses that apply. Then insist also that all members be informed in detail on the existing situation. This approach will benefit the entire hobby.

If you do acquire imports, it is important to give attention to their proper acclimatization. Birds arriving from other countries have been exposed to all manner of discomfort and danger during the trip. They will also be slow in becoming accustomed to new food sources.

Never house newly arrived birds with earlier arrivals. If they're housed in the same quarters, they could spread disease. Place the imports in separate, roomy cages and house males and females separately. The best is the so-called box cage that is well protected on all sides. Place an infrared lamp near the front. It will help those birds that "don't look so great" after a long, tiring journey, and it will also help those that appear well and in good condition. Set the lamp about 24″ (65 cm.) from the front of the cage and set things up so that the bird can move away from the heat if it so desires.

Almost all finches love panicum millet. Provide a dish of the small millet varieties, canary grass seed, weed and grass seed, and niger seed. For drinking, provide boiled tapwater; allow to cool; dissolve some disinfectant in it (ask your pet store manager to show you some bird disinfectants). I have had consistent success with fresh, cooled chamomile tea. I make it up fresh twice a day, and in the evening I replace it with boiled (and then cooled) tap water with disinfectant. Remember that chamomile tea turns sour quickly in warm weather; that's why I make it fresh twice a day.

Place drinking cups in a location where no droppings can fall into the water; not taking this precaution can lead to a lot of trouble.

Chamomile tea has a healing quality for mild intestinal and stomach disorders, even those that involve diarrhea.

After two weeks, I start providing only tap water (boiled and then cooled to room temperature). In areas with hard water, I suggest using distilled or spring water, which can be purchased in the supermarket or drug store.

Recently imported birds should not bathe the first two to three weeks. Wait till they perch healthy and lively before letting them bathe. Once again I provide tap water at room temperature for this purpose and add to it one-third part of chamomile tea cooled to the same temperature. I do this because birds like to drink before they bathe. After a week, you can omit the chamomile tea. Chamomile tea also has a healing function in the bath water. If there are any patches of inflamed skin (which can be hidden from our view by the feathers), they will disappear when exposed to chamomile tea.

Recently arrived birds will instinctively look for food on the floor. So when you provide food, sprinkle some on the floor and hang the seed dishes low in the cage and close to perches. Furnish drinking water in flat, earthenware dishes. Preferably, cover the dishes with wire mesh, so birds can't bathe in the drinking water.

For the first four days, don't feed new birds any fortified food and no green food, to avoid diarrhea. Sprouted seed, however, will be greatly appreciated.

Scatter some sand on the floor of the cage, not too sharp, and replace it daily. Or else, use grit. This helps eliminate intestinal bacteria. It can happen that recently imported birds take in too much sand or grit. If so, cover the floor with paper (not newspaper) because too large an intake of sand or grit also can cause all kinds of stomach and intestinal disorders.

Keep the cage scrupulously clean and wash all utensils at least once a day with hot water and then disinfect them.

Watch carefully for any sign of watery droppings, and if you notice it, take immediate action. This symptom can be life threatening for birds. To the drinking water add a five to ten percent glucose solution and provide some poppyseed in the normal seed mix.

I recommend providing a night light (4 to 7 watt), so that the birds can see enough to eat and drink at night if they want to. Sometimes the infrared lamp provides enough light, but if you use one, be sure to leave it on day and night.

For an antibiotic, I recommend oxytetracycline Hcl 20 percent, at a dosage of five gram per liter of drinking water for one or two weeks. Another popular antibiotic is sigmamycine (10 gram per quart of drinking water for one or two weeks).

Once you have had your recently imported birds in quarantine for two weeks, you can start offering them chickweed for green food, and also small amounts of egg food. By the way, you can commence feeding insects (ant "eggs," mealworms, white worms, fruit flies, etc.) ten days after arrival, provided the birds look chipper and healthy. But remember that any time birds are offered any new type of food, be sure to watch carefully for diarrhea; if you notice any, discontinue the new food for several weeks.

After two weeks, you can limit the use of the infrared lamp to night time. However, if you have any weak birds, keep the infrared lamp on day and night for several more weeks.

Birds become accustomed quickly to a caretaker, so during the acclimatization process, always have the same person clean the cages and provide the food and water. This helps keep things quiet, thus avoiding stress.

The acclimatization period takes about a month. After that time, you can house your birds in a roomy aviary or roomy cages. If you keep the birds out of doors, be sure not to expose them to temperatures below 72° F (22° C) at any time. Aviaries should have a protective sleeping coop (night shelter) with plenty of sleeping boxes. Cages should be moved indoors, if necessary, when evening falls. In early spring and in the fall, don't house recently acclimatized birds outside at all. And don't use the birds for breeding the first year after arrival; this would weaken them too much.

Furthermore, African and Australian Estrildines have to get used to a new succession of the seasons, for when it is summer there, it is winter here, and vice versa. Recently imported females are more likely to develop egg binding because they haven't had a chance to exercise enough during the acclimatization period.

For information on regulation of the U.S. Department of Agriculture's Animal and Plant Health Inspection Service (USDA/APHIS), contact:

Import/Export Staff
USDA, APHIS Veterinary Services
Federal Building
Hyattsville, MD 20782
Phone: 301-436-8172

If you are a pet store owner, it's important for you to be a member of the Pet Industry Joint Advisory Council (PIJAC) at 1710 Rhode Island Avenue, N.W., 2d Floor, Washington, DC 20036. (Telephone: 202-452-1525). PIJAC is a federation of leading pet industry retailers, distributors, companion animal breeders and importers, manufacturers, trade associations, and aquarium, avian and herpetological societies. Their membership consists of 32 associations, hobbyist clubs and societies (approximately 100,000 members), and over 1,000 individual and company memberships. PIJAC's members breed, acquire, import/export, transport and sell virtually every species of live animal not only as companion pets but also for zoological specimens and biomedical research.

PIJAC works extensively with federal, state and local legislative and regulatory bodies in the formulation of laws and regulations relating to companion pet animals, and supports the enactment of reasonable and rational laws and regulations that protect the health and well-being of pet animals as well as the general public. PIJAC welcomes hobbyists as members.

Accommodation

You can get to know your birds, their behavior and life experiences only if housing and care are well arranged. Good housing promotes careful observation and record keeping, and that's important for all types of birds. Don't think that because they are so common, Zebra Finches (*Taeniopygia* [*Poephila*] *guttata*) or Society Finches (*Lonchura striata var. domestica*) don't need to be observed, that nothing new could be found out about them. That's by no means the case. We need to know as many details as possible about all our birds because there already are a number of countries that forbid export of their birds (Australia, Malagasy, and others). Other nationalistic limitations can be expected, so that soon we can expect to be limited to birds that are bred in captivity. Every bit of imported breeding stock should be received and maintained with care.

Cages, Vitrines, Room or Indoor Aviaries, Outside Aviaries, Bird Houses

Most Estrildid Finches are rather small, and people are tempted to think that they can be kept in small quarters. Not so. There should always be enough room for them to exercise adequately. Small quarters lead to fat and listless birds that won't breed. This is particularly true for the Diamond Sparrow (*Stagonopleura guttata*). Even the smallest finches should be given a cage of at least 30" long × 18" wide × 20" high (75 cm. × 45 cm. × 50 cm.), and always housed in *pairs* if available.

I prefer cages that are as long as they are wide, which would change the dimensions I just mentioned to 30" × 30" (75 cm. × 75 cm.). Cages measuring 30" × 30" × 20" (75 × 75 × 50 cm.) are appropriate for two pairs, or, in a pinch, for three pairs, provided the birds are really small. At that level of crowding, don't set your sights too high for breeding results.

The best type of cage is the so-called *box cage,* which allows birds to feel the most protected and safest, as experience has shown. A box cage has wire mesh only on the front. The sides, roof, floor and rear wall can be made of wood or other material. Paint the inside of the cage with a safe, lead-free, light-colored paint. You can use paint intended for children's furniture, for example. This paint is easy to wash. For the outside, you can use any type of paint you wish. Over the floor, build a second floor of metal (zinc), hardboard, or the like, that can slide in and out. Then take a sheet of glass about 4" (10 cm.) high and put it along the entire front of the cage to prevent spills of seed hulls, sand, and feathers. Make sure that this sheet of glass is easy to remove.

In the sidewalls (and the rear-wall, too, if you like), install some doors so that you can reach all areas of the cage. Ideally, the front of the cage also should be constructed so that it can be slid open; this helps simplify feeding and watering. You can hang a bath in one of the doors, although a flat, earthenware dish set on the floor will also be appreciated.

Location of the cage is quite important. Be sure there is enough light and fresh air—but definitely no drafts! Never place a cage close to an open window because it is almost impossible to avoid a draft there. Also, a window location could expose birds to strong, direct sunlight, which can rapidly raise the temperature in the cage.

Vitrines are currently quite popular. These make fine quarters, provided they are constructed correctly and are large enough, especially for the more fragile exotics. The front is made of glass or plexiglass. The sides and roof are made partially of wire mesh; these parts should be equipped with shutters to regulate fresh air and ventilation. There should be several doors in the sides to permit all necessary tasks.

A vitrine is excellent for a living room or study. Add some suitable plants and you will have a really attractive exhibit.

You will need a thermometer to check the temperature and maintain it properly. I recommend that the glass front slope, so that the vitrine is wider at the bottom than the top. This way, droppings and dirt are less likely to spoil the view. The glass front really should be removable, so that it will slide out easily for cleaning. Make two parallel grooves on each side, so that—before removing the glass plate—you can install a solid piece of cardboard or a similarly sized piece of glass to contain the birds. The bottom also should have a floor that can slide out as with a box cage.

Equip a vitrine properly. Furnish some live branches, placed in jelly jars filled with wet sand to keep them fresh; make a wire-mesh cover, so that you can insert the branches easily. Have some containers solely for green food, and supply separate dishes for food, water, and bathing. Also install several perches separated by an appropriate distance.

Cover the floor with so-called "bird gravel" (sharp sand, charcoal, which combats hyperacidity and sweetens the stomach, and oyster shells, which supply calcium) about 1″ (4 cms.) deep, and put some small stones (flagstones and such) on top. You can backlight the vitrine if you like. Some people decorate the walls with nature scenes, but I don't recommend this. You can become bored looking at these after awhile. I suggest you use a neutral light blue or soft gray color that will show off the birds well. Use washable paint because the birds tend to splash while bathing and otherwise spread dirt. The glass front, of course, also gets dirty and you need to count on washing it at least twice a week. Birds will be less alarmed if you insert the cardboard before sliding out the glass front.

An *indoor aviary* should have a surface of at least 18″ (half meter) square. Personally, I prefer aviaries twice that size. Larger doesn't hurt. This size

Early cotoneaster.   *Photo by Ramond Gudas, courtesy Pet Age*

Japanese spirea.   *Photo by Raymond Gudas, courtesy Pet Age*

aviary can hold two to four pairs. It is large enough even for the young that you expect later. Place the entire aviary on a platform at least two feet (60 cm.) high to avoid cold drafts.

As with any type of quarters, be sure that you have access to the inside of the aviary so that you can service it for food, water, nest boxes, clean-up, etc., without disturbing the birds too much. Take this into account when you build the aviary.

A *bird room* is fun to set up, if you have the available space, especially if it has several windows facing south, southeast or southwest. Make sure the birds you house together are compatible. You must plan your collection carefully to satisfy this precondition. You want to avoid fights that cause commotion, particularly during the breeding season.

Once you have independent fledglings in the bird room, take them to other quarters because many parents have the habit of chasing their young-adult offspring around. This again disturbs the peace that you want to maintain during the breeding season.

You can split up the bird room into two, four, or six aviaries with a service aisle along the middle. This way you are able to maintain several collections and to have separate quarters available for quarrelsome birds, newly independent young, or for other reasons. It is also easier to observe your birds with such an arrangement. If you place all the birds together in one room, you usually get a situation where the aviculturist has to sit with his nose against the wire mesh on the door frame, often exposed to a drafty hallway or causeway.

Be sure to put screens on all the windows, so that you can open them safely to let in fresh air and direct sunlight. This is of prime importance for your feathered friends. Paint the walls with washable paint in natural, quiet colors, like light green, gray, pale blue, and such.

Decorate the corners with live plants in pots and barrels (see page 53), and install fabricated perches there, too. This way you preserve maximum flight space. You can consider planting elder, willow, roses, all types of philodendron, reeds, bamboo, privet, or dwarf conifers. You will have to count on some damage inflicted by the birds, so that now and then you will have to replace the plants. But actually, the damage isn't as great as you might think. You will need to spray the plants regularly with a mister. I consider a bird room complete only if proper attention has been given to plants. If you have a dense collection of plants, you have a good chance that many types of birds will build a nest there in the open, which is highly interesting in itself.

An ideal situation is to have a bird room on the ground floor with an outdoor aviary attached. This is the most appropriate set-up of all. Even if the exposure isn't ideal in such a case, I would still advise you to consider it; with the aid of glass on the outside you can correct a less than ideal exposure considerably. On pleasant, sunny, windless days, you can open the windows and the birds can enjoy fresh air and direct sunlight to their heart's content, a vital factor for exotic finches. Ultraviolet rays on the feathers are beneficial, and birds that have been kept indoors for a long winter improve visibly when they can come back out into the open air and enjoy a daily sun bath. The outdoor aviary should have plenty of plantings, also, so that birds can hide in the greens if they need to. An excess of sun is not good, either!

The *outdoor or garden aviary* is currently the most popular type of housing. As a result, you have a great variety of well-constructed aviaries to choose from. I will discuss this type of housing in special detail.

First, the size: it should be 6' high × 6' wide × 9' long, minimum (2 m. × 2 m. × 3 m.).

A more complex *bird house* is becoming common among more experienced bird fanciers. This consists of an indoor aviary (in a separate building), a quarantine room, an acclimatization room, and several attached outdoor aviaries. All these must be built and furnished in the same manner as a basic garden or outdoor aviary. I would recommend constructing the aviary relatively wider than longer. This allows young or weak birds to find a haven more easily if that becomes necessary, and you will be more able to make the necessary observations. A stretched-out aviary encourages the birds to make long flights, one after the other, and you will not be able to enjoy seeing much of their behavior and colorful appearance. A bird house is best built of masonry and should have a good number of openable windows. The windows should be covered with permanent screens to make sure the birds can't fly out when the windows are opened or hurt themselves against the glass. The inside aviary can be arranged as described above for indoor aviaries (see page 40).

A good outdoor aviary has a covered and an open section. Let us discuss the open section first. Locate the front of it toward the south as much as possible; if you need to deviate, southeast is better than southwest. Even if the front is properly oriented, I would still suggest making part of it of glass (use only non-reflecting glass). Naturally you will want to place the aviary where you can view it easily, set attractively among some flowers, plants or bushes.

From the start, plan to make the outdoor aviary attack-proof against the entry of all vermin, wildlife, and cats. Pour concrete foundation. The upright sides should be supported by metal T-beams. Wood is not so easy to make attack-proof, but if you need to use it, fortify the edges with metal. Build a wall (of brick or cinder block) on the foundation, about 12″ to 18″ high (30 to 50 cm.), on which you lay the floor. The best flooring is concrete, especially for the sleeping coop or night shelter. You can also use creosoted flooring and tiles. For solid walls or sections I suggest using tongued-and-grooved pine boards, but this can be expensive. The roof should be sloped somewhat. I recommend roof tiles. If you build the aviary against an existing wall or fence, make sure that the roof extends over the wall, so that water doesn't gather in the cracks (although you could minimize the problem with a sheet of tarpaper).

Other materials you'll need are strong wire mesh (½ × ½ inch; 25 × 25 mm), wire, nails, and glass. For the semi-covered part of the outdoor aviary, use safety glass. I recommend a good metal or plastic gutter, also.

I suggest letting the environment dictate the size of the aviary. You're not keeping chickens or ducks, where it makes sense to let the size of the flock dictate the size of the coop. See what size aviary would suit the surroundings, then decide the number of birds you can keep. If you have enough space, you can try colony breeding (with several pairs of the same species), which is recommendable for many of the exotic finches.

In designing an aviary, maintain simple lines and a construction that fits into the surroundings as much as possible. Actually, this advice also applies for other types of bird housing. The emphasis should be on the contents of the facility, and you should not install such "improvements" as projections, turrets, cupolas, and the like. Try to let the aviary blend into the environment and adapt itself to its surroundings. Strategically, place plants, bushes, and flowers in the manner described earlier.

The standard aviary has three sections: (1) A completely open section; the flight, (2) a covered section; the partially enclosed flight, and (3) a completely enclosed shelter in the form of a sleeping coop or an indoor aviary (night shelter). Sleeping quarters should always be furnished if only to have a place to install heaters and lights. The covered section should have a watertight roof. The rest of it is built from wire mesh. The floor can be sand, but a floor of cement tiles covered thickly with sand also works excellently. If you use concrete or tile floors, place the plantings in barrels. Bring in fresh willow branches, fruit-tree branches, and such, plus various dense bushes that can be replaced when necessary. Be sure to supply sufficient perches.

The open area of the aviary (the flight or run) should have perches even if you supply plenty of natural plantings to perch in. All artificial perches should be sanitized regularly. Those in the open run will, of course, be washed by the rain. When you water the plantings, you can still rinse them with a soft spray from the hose. Check their condition regularly.

The windows in the night shelter should have reinforced glass, so that the birds will notice the glass and not fly into it. Plexiglass also works well (stick some colored tape to the glass so the birds will see it).

Separate a section of the coop as an entryway with a double door, to avoid escape. When entering, close the outside door before opening the inside door that enters into the run.

The next section of the coop should have a floor half of which should be raised. The upper part is the real sleeping area. The lower part can be split into two "rooms," one to serve as a mating area, quarantine area, cooling off area for those who breach the peace, observation area, and so forth. The other section can be a storage place for nest boxes, perches, bowls, and such. The floor of this lower section is best when built of cement or tile. The floor of the sleeping quarters should be cement, covered with a layer of sand mixed with grit and oyster shells, about 2″ or 3″ thick (6 to 8 cm.).

Catching, Purchasing, and Shipping

Trying to catch an exotic finch in an enclosure is always a nervewracking task. If you do the task planfully, it will certainly go easier after you have gained some experience at it.

Get a good net with a short grip; the rim should be heavily padded. Then get some lessons from an experienced handler. See how the pet-store manager does the job and talk over his method with him.

Catching birds in a roomy aviary is easier than doing the job in a cage or small vitrine because you have more operating room. Remove all artificial perches and other utensils from the aviary before going to work because you don't want anything in your way. You'll have enough trouble with just the plants.

I catch my birds in stages when there are several to catch, as when they need to be brought indoors for the winter. As I enter the aviary, a number of birds naturally fly off into the sleeping coop. I close the door on them, and go to work on the birds that remain in the run. When I have caught them, I open the sleeping coop again, step inside, and let another group of birds fly into the run. I close the door once more and catch those birds. I keep up this routine till I have caught all my birds. I always catch them in flight, not on a perch.

Be sure that you don't have a net with too large a mesh because the birds can get terribly tangled. If that ever happens, it causes a real strain on your nerves, not to speak of the effect on the birds before they are properly disentangled.

When examining birds you're considering buying, never put your nose right up against the wire mesh of the cage holding a bird you're interested in. Even if the bird is at death's door, it will sit straight and hold its feathers in tight when it suddenly sees a human face several inches away. Rather, do your inspection at a good distance.

Don't be taken in by sales talk. Birds that have puffed up feathers or are easily caught by hand are at best dubious cases; don't listen to talk that these are just "tame" or "friendly."

Do take in your hand a bird that interests you. Blow aside some breast feathers and check that the breast is meaty and full. Look at the legs; they should be smooth, not scaly. The beak should look normal and the eyes should be clear and bright.

Once you decide to buy, put the bird promptly in a shipping cage. Wrap the cage in newspaper or packing-paper and head for home as quickly as possible. The shipping cage doesn't have to be fancy for a short trip. You can safely carry several finches together in a shoebox in which you have poked some ventilation holes.

If you need to ship birds a considerable distance by commercial carrier, find out what type of container is required by the carrier. Generally they prefer flat, wooden shipping cages with a small strip of wire mesh in the front. It is equipped with a round perch and two compartments for seed and wet bread. (You don't want to put water inside because it would spill in transit.) Wrap the cage in thick paper and poke some holes in it for ventilation. That will let in some light but keep it dark enough to help quiet the birds. In bright cages they tend to fly around. I suggest you pad the inside of the top of the cage with foam rubber to avoid injury if birds do fly up.

Mark the outside of the cage with labels indicating "*Live Birds,*" "*Handle with Care,*" "*Don't Drop,*" "*Don't Bump,*" and "*This Side Up*" (with an arrow). You probably can get them from the carrier for the asking; if not, make them yourself.

Be sure to check ahead of time on the shipping rules of the carrier you intend to use. Many airlines allow you to take a single pet into the cabin with you, provided you can fit the cage under your seat. You'll probably have to make reservations ahead of time and generally you'll have to pay an extra charge.

If you have several birds, or large birds, they'll have to travel in the cargo hold. Be sure to wrap the cage well in such cases because the temperature in the cargo hold can drop severely. I would line the entire inside of the shipping cage with indoor/outdoor carpeting.

Don't cage birds together if they are at all likely to harm each other. Don't overcrowd the shipping cage. Group birds of similar size together to avoid the danger of big birds pushing the little ones against the wall, which can have serious consequences.

If someone ships birds to you, be especially cautious when this is done in winter. Cold temperatures cause the temperature to drop inside the hollow bone structure of the birds. You have the natural tendency to put a cold bird up close to a toasty heater, but actually that is the most dangerous thing you could do. The air in the bones expands in response to the sudden increase in temperature, which causes the birds a lot of pain. It could kill them.

In making shipping arrangements, remember that exotic finches need to eat every single day, and they should always have access to seed and water.

New arrivals should not be put into the aviary right away; keep them separate in a location where the temperature is pleasant and where they can recover from the journey in peace. Feed them generously, using food sent along by the seller. Then, gradually convert to your own menu if this happens to be different (and better!). Also, don't forget to offer drinking water (room temperature). Keep the birds warm with an infrared lamp and keep a close eye on them.

If you buy birds close to home, transport them early in the day so that they can use the rest of the day to become adjusted to their new environment.

When the time comes to integrate new birds into the rest of your collection, place the newcomers' cage and all into the aviary. Keep them inside the cage half a day, from about 7 a.m. to 1 p.m. This way the birds can get used to one another before you release the newcomers. Then watch the situation closely. It can happen that the established group will not accept the newcomers, seeing them as a challenge to their territory.

Watch what happens for a few days; if the rejection continues, remove the new birds and then reintroduce them gradually after another few days have passed. Generally, new birds won't cause problems in the aviary, provided it isn't overcrowded. Be aware, of course, that you shouldn't introduce new birds during the breeding season. You are really asking for trouble if you do that!

If you have new birds in the aviary, place water and spread some seed here and there on the aviary floor because finches instinctively look for food on or near the ground. Keep this up until you are sure that the newcomers have found the food bowls. The old birds show the new ones by their actions where to find food and water, and they learn by example.

A final word of advice on escapes. I have mentioned that the aviary should have a safety porch. Still it can happen that a bird escapes. If it is one of a pair, then it shouldn't ordinarily be difficult to catch the escapee. Use a cage with a trap door and put the remaining partner of the pair in the closed part of the cage. Then put some seed in the part with the trap door. The bird in the cage will send out contact calls and it won't be long till the escaped bird is attracted to the cage. First of all, it ordinarily won't have flown far from the aviary. When it observes its partner in the cage and if it discovers food in the cage as well, it will return to captivity quickly. Even if the escapee isn't paired, another bird of the same species can still serve as "bait." If two paired birds both escape, the situation is a bit more difficult. Still the process is the same. You put another bird of the same species in the trap cage to attract one of the escaped birds, which then in turn serves as "bait" for the other.

If you don't have any success with the trap cage you have to wait until evening or night-time. Note precisely where the escaped finch goes to sleep. Then shine a flashlight directly at the escaped bird. The sharp light seems to freeze the roosting bird in its resting place and you can lift it off the branch by hand.

If a finch escapes from a cage, it is often enough to remove all other inhabitants temporarily from that cage and set it outside, with the door(s) open. Hunger and thirst will tend to drive the escapee back to the trusted cage after a few hours to take advantage of the feed and water it finds there.

Equipping Facilities for Exotic Finches

You should get two different types of perches: anchored ones and swinging ones. The swinging perches are for play, the anchored ones are for resting and for mating during the breeding season.

Aviaries with good plantings naturally provide perches in a variety of branches for sitting and sleeping. Many species of birds will even build nests in the plantings. Natural roosts are especially popular in summer, but I still recommend furnishing separate sleeping quarters. In the indoor aviary, provide anchored, round perches; likewise for the covered part of an outdoor or garden aviary. In other parts of the outdoor aviary, you can provide sleeping boxes in wind- and draft-free locations.

Perches should be made of hardwood dowels and slightly flattened on top. Hardwood is recommended because it is less likely to harbor lice and mites. The perches should not be too thin. They must be thick enough to keep the toes of resting birds from closing around them completely. Otherwise the birds can't relax well. I suggest you get perches of different diameter. These keep toe nails trim and leg muscles limber.

Don't skimp on places to perch and sleep. You don't want your birds to get into fights over them. Don't install one perch on top of another. You don't want birds perching above to foul the ones below. For the same reason, don't install perches over food and water bowls and baths.

For natural perches, I recommend branches from fruit trees, willow, elderberry and sycamore. Remember to replace them regularly, because after awhile, cut branches lose their elasticity. If you have birds that have quick-growing nails, I recommend reeds and similar plants that help keep their nails trim. Rough stones (flagstones) serve the same purpose.

Furnish the garden aviary, further, with plants (see page 53). First of all, this will give it a natural appearance. Second, it provides nesting places. Third, the plants attract all types of small creatures, like aphids, spiders, bugs, and others. This comes in handy especially at breeding time, when most birds absolutely require them for the proper feeding of the young. Observations in the wild and examinations of bird crops have shown that the young even of seedeating finches are fed almost exclusively on insects and spiders during the first period of their lives.

Many plants you can consider for the garden aviary also have the advantage of providing berries—as elder, cotoneaster, and firethorn. Birds love the berries. The only disadvantage of planting live bushes in the garden aviary is that they take up a relatively large amount of space that otherwise could be used as flight space for the birds. Besides, several types of birds tend to be hard on bushes and they can look pretty rough even after a short time.

Years of experimenting led by my friend E. P. J. Meijer to a satisfactory solution for minimizing the drawbacks of live bushes in finch aviaries by using firethorn exclusively. Firethorn (*Pyracantha coccinea*) has the advantage that it can be trellised, meaning that the branches can be led along walls and fences. It works particularly well along a closed (rear) wall. If the rear side is made of stone or solid wood it is easier to train the firethorn along its expanse. Plant the firethorn as close to the wall as possible. Then, spread the branches against the wall and attach them. Resistant branches can be cut close to the stem. This way, you train a plant to grow tightly against the wall. If you keep attaching new growth consistently, it won't be long until the wall is completely covered. After awhile, this "living wall" can become a foot (30 cm.) thick. You can place sleeping and breeding boxes between the branches. Training branches takes extra work and patience, but it is worth the trouble.

In May and June the firethorn will reward you with countless white blossoms that resemble those of the better-known hawthorn. These fragrant blossoms attract countless flies and other bugs that are hunted down by many birds. In the summer, the berries start to form, and by fall they will ripen and your back aviary wall will be festooned in glowing red, orange, or yellow, depending on the variety you planted. The ripe berries contain many small pits, which provide a welcome addition to the menu of the birds as soon as they become used to the taste.

Canaries and parakeets need to be kept away from the firethorn because they gnaw too much. (I don't recommend that you keep parakeets in the same aviary with exotic finches, anyway!) If you want to protect the firethorn, build a second "rear wall" about 2" (5 cm.) in front of your "firethorn wall." Make this second wall of so-called parakeet mesh, which is one mesh size bigger than the half-inch mesh. The majority of the tropical finches are small enough to get through the mesh and enjoy the firethorn, while the somewhat larger canaries and parakeets are limited to gnawing on whatever branches project from the wall and grow through the wire-mesh second wall. But, again, it is inadvisable to house parakeets and canaries in an aviary with finches.

In case you're concerned about the thorns of the firethorn, this is no problem for small finches. (Thorn birds exist only in legends.) I have never come across an instance where finches hurt themselves on the thorns even though they often like to take a rapid dive into a firethorn branch. You, however, *should* take precautions. When you train the branches, always wear gardening gloves because you could get scratched painfully by the thorns.

If you want to do something special, you could try decorating the open run of the garden aviary with tall-growing decorative grasses or reeds. Reeds, for example, combine well with a small pond. Ponds are fine, provided you take precautions against drownings, particularly of fledglings. Make sure that the pond has extremely shallow spots that are at the most an inch (2 cm.) deep. You can create these shallows with flagstones, other flat stones, or gravel. Also, build the sides with a long slope, so that a bird that falls in can get out again easily. Finally, be sure that you install a drain at the deepest point of the pond. You need it in order to freshen the water and clean the pond. For this reason, construct the pond on the highest spot in the aviary, if possible, and attach a garden hose to the drain, so that you can lead the waste water away from the aviary.

Utensils come in many shapes, sizes and colors. The best ones are made of white porcelain or hard plastic, are oval, and measure about 4" (10 cm.) in diameter. You can consider automatic feeders, provided they really work well. Automatic waterers or drinking vessels are good, too, and are really better than bowls because birds can't foul them. Large, glazed bowls or plastic containers are useful for sprouted seeds, universal food, and other supplements that are provided in small quantities to prevent spoilage. Separate vessels for grit and oyster shell must also be provided. Use flat bowls for bird

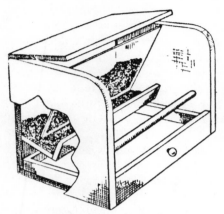

Seed feeder for mixed seeds.

Seed feeder in which the seeds can be offered separately.

Drinking vessel.

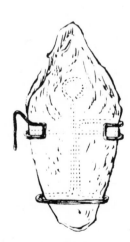

Cuttlebone.

baths. If you don't have them, you can adapt deeper bowls by putting flat stones or gravel in them. You want to prevent drowning, particularly of young birds.

In cages, insert all utensils in the sides and in door openings or specially made openings. The well-known plastic food dispenser that hangs against the door is a good example.

In aviaries, put utensils close to a door, near the nest—but not too close, to minimize the chance of escape and of attack by cats. Again, this is for your convenience, to check on the food supply and to add to it without causing unnecessary disturbance. Do check on the utensils daily. Fill food bowls daily and put fresh, clean water in dishes and bird baths several times daily.

Most exotic finches don't like to stay on the ground if they don't have to, except to drink. Therefore, build a platform about 30″ (75 cm.) off the ground to put feeding dishes on. Bottle-shaped automatic waterers can be hung up; they will be well used. In larger aviaries, build several feeding platforms to minimize fighting at the food dishes. The platform should have a 4″ rim (10 cm.) to keep the dishes from sliding off.

Place grit, limestone and other supplements in separate vessels. Cuttle bone is provided and hung against the outside wall of the sleeping shelter. During the breeding season hang small baskets with nest-building material in the same place. Don't just put supplies on the ground; this gives the aviary an unattractive appearance. You can also buy special racks for providing green food. Branches (with aphids!) and bunches of weeds (for seeds) can be put in deep flower pots filled with wet sand.

Provide good lighting, particularly in the sleeping coop. Finches are just plain lovers of light. In fall and winter, when it gets dark early, provide extra light so that birds can continue to eat and drink. Exotic finches should have at least 10-13 hours of light each day. Also, install a small night light (4 to 7 watt) in the sleeping coop, so that birds that fly up when they are startled can find their sleeping spot again. When you turn off the lights, dim them gradually.

A heater that can provide the required temperature safely is very important! In the detailed section on the various exotic finches, I'll indicate precise temperature requirements. Most species cannot tolerate temperatures below 50° F (10° C). Keep alert to the weather forecast, a suggestion I shared earlier.

Make It True To Nature

If you're planning to set up an aviary, make it as true to nature as possible by adding a few good bushes.

Finches use plants to play in, as shelter from the rain, to shade themselves from strong sunlight, or just to perch in. In addition, natural perches play an important role at mating time, and bushes also provide good nesting places.

Obviously, you should select sturdy bushes that will tolerate your birds' gnawing. Actually, you can considerably reduce the tendency of birds to destroy vegetation by regularly (preferably every day) furnishing fresh green food (see page 81).

I do not mean to imply that birds will leave bushes entirely untouched, even if you have extensive planting. That would be far from the truth. Many larger finches, for example, have a lust for the buds of the common privet, and most birds like the berries, leaves or buds of ivy, holly, bird cherry and elder. Still, you can minimize the damage to growing plants by furnishing fresh greens daily.

Planting takes planning. For example, don't plant rhododendrons in aviaries housing hookbills like parrots and parakeets. These inveterate gnawers could be poisoned by the leaves of this plant. For other birds, hence all finches, rhododendrons are no problem.

There should also be a patch of grass in every aviary. It's decorative, but it's also a necessity for species like quail, who "weave" a tunnel through long grass in which they nest; all Australian grass finches love to search for insects in grass, while many African finches just like to sit in it, taking a sun bath. Larger finch species also value the grass patch. You will see them after a rain, rolling enthusiastically through the wet grass, all the while screeching exuberantly.

Consider planting rushes and corn plants in one of the corners of the aviary. Mannikins and other *Lonchura* species, among many others, really appreciate these plants, and they help control the nail growth of these birds. Also plant some conifers and trees of the *Prunus* species—sturdy ones that don't grow too high. They are especially appropriate for a garden aviary of small exotics!

It's a good idea to get advice from a gardener or nursery before placing plants in the aviary. Not every type of soil is suitable for the plants I am recommending.

It's equally important to maintain the plantings, or you run the risk that the place will become overgrown. Trim plants regularly and consult gardening books for proper maintenance.

A LARGE SELECTION

Here are some aviary plants worthy of serious consideration:

American Arbor Vitae *(Thuja occidentalis)*

This is a good hedge, especially for a community aviary of small tropical birds. The scallop-shaped leaves are placed in a cross design, while the twigs are dark green on top and light green on the bottom. The tree can grow as tall as 50' (15 meters). It is a native of North America that has had wide acceptance elsewhere. Plant only young ones.

Austrian Pine *(Pinus nigra)*

This is frequently used in decorative plantings and can be found in some woods where it has been purposely introduced. It has needles that grow two by two and can be up to 6″ (15 cm.) long. Greenish-black in color, the young plants in particular are quite decorative. Many finches like to build their nests in pines, especially if you help them get started with a base of woven rope (or the like) placed between the branches or in a fork. I've seen this plant used effectively against a cement back wall, as long as it is trimmed to keep it low.

Bamboo *(Sinarundinaria)*

Purchased at better florists and garden centers, bamboo is not always easy to get started in aviaries, but if planted successfully, it is quite decorative. Mannikins and other small finches whose nails tend to grow fast like to frequent bamboo. It is preferable to place this plant around a little pond in the open flight, where the soil is moist and where there is shade for a good part of the day. Bamboo can be propagated by removing some shoots and replanting them.

Beech *(Fagus sylvatica)*

A beech tree is especially useful in aviaries that are part of a large garden, particularly if the birds have access to an open run. When fully grown, the tree can provide needed shade. It is generally best not to grow a beech in an enclosed aviary because it grows too large, up to 100′ high (30 m.). For an enclosed aviary, I'd recommend a European hornbeam.

Boxwood (Buxus sempervirens)

This boxwood originally came from the area around the Mediterranean Sea. It is an evergreen, and for that reason alone it would be good for an aviary. The leaves are oval, grow to less than one inch (2 cm.), and have a leathery feel. They are dark green on top and light green on the bottom. Boxwoods do especially well as a strip of hedge about 3′ (one meter) in length. Many tropical and subtropical finches (and other bird species) like to build nests in boxwood hedges, particularly the various types of Australian grass finches and Weaver birds.

Broom *(Sarothamnus scoperius)*

This shrub can frequently be found on barren, sandy soils. It has branched shoots that are green in color and showy yellow flowers that appear in May. Once it has finished blooming, flat black pods appear. You can cut the bushes, tie them together loosely and attach them to the roof of the aviary. Hollow the sheaf out a little, and the birds will love to build nests in it. You can plant wild and cultivated broom in the aviary, and it will do quite well if it gets full sun. Broom requires a sandy, acid soil.

Buddleia *(Buddleia davidii)*

This shrub can grow up to a height of 13' (four meters) or more, but young plants are certainly worth planting in an aviary. Birds like it for nest building, for resting, or for an overnight shelter. To keep the shrub from growing too large, cut it back to a height of about 10" (25 cm.) each year. The flowers of the shrub appear in June and look like lilacs. The shrub attracts countless insects, including some that birds relish.

Climbing Rose *(Rosa multiflora)*

The climbing rose is excellently suited to an aviary. The small leaves are unevenly feathered, sharply serrated, and oval in shape. Stems grow along the ground, or climb upward, and have saber-like thorns that grow in pairs. The plant makes an unusually good hedge and therefore is quite suited to a roomy group aviary. Actually, you can use all types of cultivated roses inside and around the aviary. They give extra color and life to your collection. In addition, many types of roses are quite susceptible to aphids, which provide a special feast for the finches.

Cotoneaster

I recommend the use of this richly branched shrub. It demands little and doesn't take up much of the garden. There are a number of types, evergreen as well as deciduous. There are also dwarf and tall varieties. The type of cotoneaster you buy and the location in which you place it determine the time it will flower, either April or May. The flowers are rather small and range from white to pale red in color. The shrub produces pitted red fruits that are a treat to fruit-eating birds, particularly the thrushes; larger finch species also like them. Cotoneaster is one of the best of the low-growing shrubs.

Douglas Fir *(Pseudotsuga taxifolia)*

Suitable for an open aviary, this tree has needles about an inch long (18-33 cm.). Arranged in double rows, they are an attractive light green on top and a grayish-green on the bottom. This fir can grow extremely tall—300' (90 m.) or more—and the trunk can be 13' (4 m.) thick. The tree is native to North America, but is widely grown elsewhere. Select young plants.

English Hawthorn *(Crataegus monigyna)*

This low, deciduous shrub has a tight network of branches that many birds like to use for nesting. The leaves have three to seven lobes and are

55

indented quite sharply. It also has red, almost bullet-shaped berries that are popular with the birds. The shrub is easy to grow; a sunny location is preferable.

English Holly *(Ilex aquifolium)*

This evergreen is a bush that can grow into a tree up to 25' (7 m.) tall. It is extremely well-suited to all types of outside aviaries. The leaves are up to 3" (7 cm.) long, have short stems, and are elliptical or oval in shape. They are green in color and have sharply pointed lobes on the edges.

Holly can adapt to the wild, being found in woods and in large, abandoned gardens, but you need both male and female bushes to produce the scarlet-red berries that are so loved by birds. Displaying flowers that are small and short-stemmed, this shrub does very well in sunny locations, particularly if the soil is acidic and not too dry.

European Elderberry *(Sambucus nigra)*

This shrub grows well and has fragrant, bunched flowers. The leaves are unevenly feathered and dark green in color. Berries are black and are readily eaten by all types of birds (not to mention humans). Another important characteristic of elderberries is that they attract aphids. If birds have access to the shrubs, they will scour them for apids and small spiders. Otherwise, you can provide your birds many hours of pure joy by cutting down several aphid-infested branches and putting them in the aviary. This is particularly good to do at breeding time—actually, it is essential for tropical and subtropical finches!

The fact that the elderberry is a sturdy shrub makes it fairly resistant to the gnawing of birds. It will grow well in the aviary that has fertile soil and plenty of water.

European Hornbeam *(Carpinus betulus)*

This is truly an ideal plant for the aviary, especially because birds love to nest in it. It has oval leaves with short stems that are clearly double-serrated. In the fall, the leaves turn an attractive brownish-yellow. They tend to stay on the shrub for a relatively long time, giving birds some protection against wind and rain. When there is a heavy frost, the leaves drop off rapidly. A hornbeam can grow into a tree reaching 45' (14 m.) in height.

European Larch *(Larix decidua)*

This tree is suited to aviaries, including those with poor soil, and so is widely used. It has light green, flexible needles that fall off in autumn. They grow in small bundles from a beaker-shaped sheath up to one inch (30 mm.) long.

Austrian pine.

Photo by Raymond Gudas, courtesy, Pet Age

Douglas fir.

Photo by Raymond Gudas, courtesy Pet Age

Boxwood.

Photo by Raymond Gudas, courtesy Pet Age

False Spirea *(Sorbaria sorbifolia)*

This shrub, originally from Siberia, can grow up to 10′ (3 m.) tall. For the aviary, use only dwarf varieties. The leaves are unevenly feathered, and the basal leaves are lancetshaped. The yellow flowers grow in sturdy, cone-shaped bunches. The shrub adapts to all types of soil, as long as it is kept fairly moist, so be sure to water it regularly. The related *Sorbaria aucupavia* is also frequently grown in aviaries; its berries are a special attraction and are avidly eaten by birds, particularly thrushes, larger finches and related friends.

Golden Laburnum *(Laburnum)*

The main reason for mentioning the Golden Laburnum in this list is to warn you to avoid it, even though it is very popular in ordinary gardens and parks. Both the leaves and the pods are poisonous!

Hydrangea *(Hydrangea)*

A hydrangea can add considerable color to your plantings with its canopy of pink, blue, or white flowers. For some reason, this plant has lost a lot of its popularity; actually, it is quite prolific and can be grown in sandy soil, provided it is well-tilled with peat moss. It should not, however, be planted in direct sunlight.

Ivy *(Hedera helix)*

This climbing evergreen is attractive and quite useful. In the wild, it is found climbing up oaks and beeches, but I have often seen it used effectively in an aviary against a stone or cement fence, on which it climbs wonderfully. The leaves of young shoots and the runners that grow along the ground can be three- or five-lobed. On the actual branches, the leaves become oval, diamond-shaped, or lancet-shaped. They feel somewhat leathery, and the veins show white in a so-called hand shape. Ivy has round, blueblack berries, and many birds eat them avidly. Tropical finches will nest in ivy, especially if some rope is wound between the branches to provide a nesting base.

Japanese Spirea *(Spirea japonica)*

This shrub is considered an ideal plant for the aviary because it has a thickly branched type of growth. The leaves fall off in autumn. As its name indicates, the shrub originated in Japan, but it is now available from any garden center. The leaves are elliptical, with a wedge-shaped base. They grow some 4″ long and up to an inch wide (10 cm. × 4 cm.). Many birds like to construct their nests in this shrub.

Jasmine *(Philadelphus)*

Jasmine is a widely appreciated plant, not only for its white blossoms, which can be single or double, but also for its strong, yet appealing fragrance. Several types are available commercially. The bush has few restrictions as far as the types of soil it will tolerate, although it should be fertilized from time to time (only with manure), and it should be located in a sunny area. Birds like to flit in and out of the branches.

Juniper *(Juniperus communis)*

This evergreen shrub can grow up to 33' (10 m.) and more, displaying fanciful forms. It makes the landscape more appealing, whether it be a wooded, open-field, or man-made environment. The less varied forms of the bush are best for the aviary. The needles stand in a wreathlike array, three by three, and are dagger-shaped. The shrub will grow well, even in somewhat sandy soil. Birds often build nests in it, or use it simply to spend the night.

Lilac *(Syringa)*

The lilac can be made to grow as a bush or tree. It tends to grow tall quickly, so it may be better to place it outside the aviary rather than in it—for example, next to the sleeping coop. In a large flight, however, lilacs shouldn't be a problem.

Lilacs blossom in May or June. The plant demands much sun and a well-limed soil. It must be fertilized each year (manure only), and the beautiful flower should be cut after it has finished blooming. There are several cultivated varieties available.

Nordmann Fir *(Abies nordmanniana)*

This fir makes an ideal aviary plant in its immature stage. It originated in Asia Minor and the Caucasus, but is now widely distributed. It has showy, shiny needles approximately an inch long (3 cm.), and these are set in a brush form. Like the silver fir, the Nordmann has egg-shaped knobs that do not hold any resin.

Oriental (or Chinese) Cedar *(Thuja orientalis)*

This tree is related to the American arbor vitae, and its leaves are arranged in a similar manner. Birds enjoy nesting in this tree, particularly if several (at least three) are planted close together, forming a large, interlocked hedge. Breeding birds feel safe and secluded there. The tree, whose needles are green on both sides, originated in Japan and China, but is widely grown in other countries. It makes few demands as far as soil type is concerned, but it does require good, regular watering.

Oregon holly grape.

Photo by Raymond Gudas,
courtesy Pet Age

Rhododendron.

Photo by Raymond Gudas, courtesy Pet Age

Oregon Holly Grape *(Mahonia aquifolium)*

This North American evergreen shrub has been widely planted in other countries. It doesn't grow more than 3′ (one meter) in height and is therefore the perfect size for an aviary. Birds love its round, dark blue berries. The leaves are unevenly feathered, indented with sharp points, and ovate to elliptical in shape. In the summer, the leaves are bright red; in the winter, black-red. The shrub can be grown in almost any location and soil type, but does require a large amount of water on a regular basis.

Privet, Common *(Liguster vulgare)*

The common privet originated in southern Europe and Asia Minor, and is generally deciduous. Its leaves are sturdy, oblong, lancet-shaped, and about 3″ (8 cm.) long. Many large parakeets, cockatiels, canaries and large finches like to eat the leaves and/or buds, which are a good supplement to their regular diet. Tropical birds, and finches in particular, consider this plant an ideal location for breeding, and canaries and large finches like to spend time in privets on sunny days. The shrub flowers in April or May, showing small, whitish flowers that grow in rather tight clusters. The wood is hard.

The privet is one of the most popular aviary plants. In a well-limed soil, the plant does exceptionally well. The "pied" privet also performs admirably; it can be used as a hedge or as a solitary plant.

Pyracantha *(Pyracantha)*

If you have a cement wall on your aviary, pyracantha is one of the plants that will grow against it quite well. The plant has white flowers that are followed by red berries, the latter being a special taste treat for your birds. It can form a dense growth that makes a good nesting place for large finches, thrushes and related species.

Red Ribes *(Ribes sanguineum)*

This shrub is highly recommended as an aviary plant, if only for its bright red berries. It can reach a height of 8′ (3 m.) and more. It also flowers early, and if the weather cooperates, pink to red flowers appear in true clusters to make the plant look and smell most lovely. This plant doesn't have complex requirements and grows in almost any type of soil. It does require partial sun.

Rhododendron *(Rhododendron ponticum)*

There are many species of rhododendron, all quite decorative. The leaves are quite tough, so they don't pose a danger for tropical finches and canaries. Rhododendrons, however, are not suitable for parrots and parakeets. These birds are attracted to the leaves, which are poisonous. Research has shown this to be true for almost all species of rhododendron, but this does not pose a danger in a community garden aviary with just canaries, tropical finches and other small birds. Rhododendrons generally keep their leaves during the winter, so birds that winter outdoors can find an ideal shelter in them.

Rhododendrons prefer acidy soil. With some extra care, the plant grows into a tight structure, allowing many birds to nest in it. The plant must be watered regularly if it is placed in the covered section of the aviary and should be fertilized with some manure from time to time. Wild rhododendrons are often used as foundation plants, just like the Oregon holly grape discussed earlier. That is certainly one of the reasons the plants are so common, especially in large aviaries with a mixed bird population. In addition to the basic purple flowers, there are white and other varieties. Rhododendrons can also be used to plant around the aviary, further adding to the variety of color.

Russian Vine (Polygonum baldschuanicum)

This climbing shrub is tough and will grow well even under adverse conditions. The branches start out red in color, but eventually become light brown. The leaves are smooth, long, ovate, and have sharp points on the ends. The branches must be trained, as they do not attach themselves without aid. The flowers are rather unimposing and look somewhat like small feathers.

The plant grows fast and must be regularly trimmed short, although you can let it go a bit in spring. Birds will quickly learn their way among the twigs and will even nest in them. The plant loses its leaves in fall, making that the best time to prune it. It will grow in any type of soil.

Silver Fir (Abies alba)

This evergreen tree is quite popular and, especially in its youthful stage, quite decorative. The needles, shiny dark green on top with two bluish stripes on the bottom, are about one inch long (2 cm.) and arranged singly. The light brown knobs on the trunk don't feel sticky, since they don't exude resin. This tree is quite adaptable and will do well even in sandy soil.

Snowberry (Symphoricarpus albus)

This shrub is a native of North America. It grows to a height of approximately 6' (2 m.). The leaves, which drop off in the fall, are round, elliptical or ovate and have short stems. The shrub has round, white berries that stay on the bush, even in winter. Blackbirds, pheasants and large quail like to eat the berries. Many tropical birds like to nest in these shrubs.

Spruce Fir (Picea excelsa)

The dark green needles of this popular evergreen, which grow to about one inch (2 cm.), are individually arrayed on the branch. Branches grow all the

Snowberry.

Photo by Raymond Gudas, courtesy Pet Age

Virburnus opulus.

Photo by Raymond Gudas, courtesy Pet Age

63

way up and down the characteristically straight trunk, especially if the tree is planted in full sunlight. Even in poor soil, the tree does well.

Viburnum species

Shrubs of this family, which is quite large, have been used in aviaries, although I don't recommend any of them for that purpose. I particularly counsel against using the well-known *Viburnus opulus,* a deciduous shrub that can grow up to 10' (3 m.) tall. Besides being too tall, it is poisonous to birds. Many of them stay away from this bush instinctively, but I wouldn't chance it under any circumstances. The berries are a shiny, transparent red and hang down in bunches. The leaves and bark are poisonous as well.

You can consider Viburnum for *outside* the aviary, because they attract all kinds of insects that can be expected to pass into the aviary to be caught and eaten by its inhabitants. The shrub requires a somewhat moist soil and a shady location.

Willow *(Salix)*

There are many species of willow, and any of them can serve as an aviary plant. They can be bushes or trees. If you keep parrots and/or parakeets, in particular, you should not pass up the opportunity to place a willow in the aviary—even a dead stump will do. Hookbills just love to hack and gnaw at the wood, and they like the bark. Many species, such as Love Birds (*Agapornidae*), use willow bark for constructing their nests. Willows thrive in moist, loose soil, and they need to be trimmed. If you keep hookbills, you should at least furnish some fresh-cut willow branches every day. Many finches like to nest in willow bushes.

Group Housing

Certain bird species can be kept together, others cannot. In the detailed descriptions that follow these introductory chapters I'll indicate whether the finches under discussion are prone to fight, and if so, when. Often you can safely house pairs of different species together, but you may have war when you house finches of the same species together, especially if you put only two pairs together. However, if you put three or more pairs together, many species, such as the Zebra Finch (*Taeniopygia* [*Poephila*] *guttata*) and the Java Sparrow (*Paddy oryzivora*) will live together in harmony. Guard carefully, on the other hand, against placing an extra male into the collection. And don't bring new birds into the community in midseason, because this will upset the territories the various pairs have established, with resulting ill effects. (Yes, aviary birds *do* establish territories!)

In this connection, watch your birds carefully. If you notice any fights of consequence or wild chases, you will know that there are bad actors in the group and you should remove the culprits immediately.

As a general rule, you can assume that birds originating from the same country are most likely to get along.

The biggest bully among exotic finches is, without doubt, the Crimson Finch (*Neochmia phaeton*). The male is aggressive not only during the breeding season but at other times as well. He even attacks his own mate frequently outside the breeding season. To others of his species he is everything but friendly and gentle. In Australia, where the Crimson Finch takes up a large habitat, he doesn't hesitate to attack birds five or more times his size, and he knows how to scare the devil out of them if they invade his territory. Also watch out for the following troublemakers: all species of Mannikins (Genus *Lonchura*), Diamond Finch (*Emblema [Zonaeginthus] guttata*), Cut-throat Finch (*Amadina fasciata*), Melba Finch (*Pytilia melba*), Red-headed Finch (*Amadina erythrocephala*), Masked Finch (*Poephila personata*), Black-breasted Fire Finch (*Lagonosticta rufopicta*), Orange-winged Pytilia (*Pytilia afra*), Java Sparrow (*Paddy oryzivora*), and Zebra Finch (*Taeniopygia [Poephila] guttata*), among others.

Chores for the Aviculturist

Daily, provide fresh and generous supplies of food, drinking water, bath water, and, during the breeding season, nesting material and good lighting and heating. All utensils for eating, drinking and bathing must be cleaned and disinfected. Also, check if there are any sick birds or provokers of unrest.

Weekly, clean cages and aviaries, except during the breeding season. During this period wait and observe the right time to clean up, with consideration for birds that are brooding and youngsters about to leave the nest. The task involves replacing sand, cleaning and sanding perches (use rough sand paper), and replacing loose, natural perches. Live plants must be rinsed, trimmed, or replaced as necessary.

Monthly, do a close and careful check on the birds and carefully check their quarters for vermin. Check toe nails and clip them if necessary. Rake the sand and replace it as necessary when the flooring is made of concrete or tile. Grassy areas must be resodded as needed.

Semiannually, disinfect the entire facility, timed before and after the breeding season. Clean and disinfect all sleeping- and nesting-boxes. When possible, replace components that are broken and burn them. Disinfect the aviary and check for breaches in the mesh and wooden partitions and posts. Consider replacing perches and planting.

In general, it is best to set definite days on the calendar for all tasks to be done; that way, you won't forget something important. Feed birds at the same time each day so they can get used to a routine. The best feeding time is about 7 or 8 A.M. Keep up the schedule even when you're not there by telling the substitute caretaker when to do what. Be particular about the feeding schedule, because birds shouldn't have to wait for their food just because you're not there. It can happen when birds are feeding their young that they stop doing so if the caretaker is several hours late with rearing food or other special food you're furnishing for feeding the young. Also, during the breeding season, things have to be managed as quietly as possible. Bring in food and water quickly but gently; the same goes for other chores on your list.

Lonchura (Euodice) cantans.

3

Common Illnesses and Their Treatment

OFTEN THE FIRST SIGN THAT BIRDS ARE SICK is listless behavior at the feeding station, where they drop more food than they eat. In most cases, you will also notice swollen or dull eyes. You'll also frequently notice puffed-up feathers. Sick birds often look like pitiful balls of feathers cowering in a corner or under a food trough, sleeping with the head buried deeply in the feathers. Their breathing is rapid.

Your first action should be to remove the bird, and keep it separate in a heated hospital cage. Then look for remedies.

A hospital cage is completely closed, except for the front, which has wire mesh. You even can cover the front with a cloth, if that seems advisable. Put a dark, infrared lamp of 75, 150, or 250 watts, at a distance of 12″ to 18″ (30 to 50 cm.) from the hospital cage. Check with your hand to make sure that the inside of the cage isn't getting too hot.

The well-known aviculturist, the late Mr. C. af Enehjelm designed a cage 14″ × 7″ × 12″ high (35 × 17 × 30 cm. high). He separated the cage into one large living area and a small "basement" 4″ deep (10 cm.), which was covered with asbestos on all sides. In the rear wall of this "basement" he placed three lamps, with switches on the outside. Along the sides, he attached three slats that permitted sliding several floors into the cage. The lowest floor consisted of a sheet of asbestos with various holes drilled into it; next came a frame holding a linen cloth to catch droppings and dirt; finally came a grate on which a bird could rest without the possibility of fouling itself in its own droppings. The

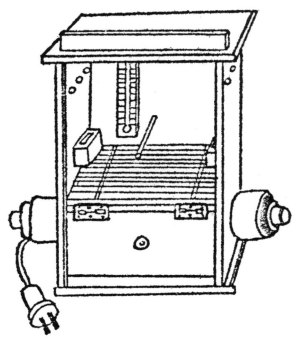

Hospital cage. The hospital cage is designed to isolate and monitor sick birds. It provides necessary warmth so important to the recovery of many birds from a variety of illnesses.

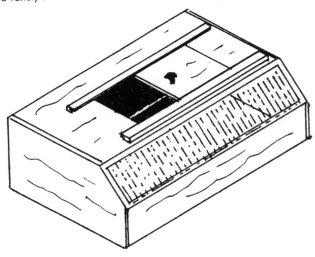

A travel cage should be constructed so that the birds are as safe from fright or injury as possible while so confined.

living space had two perches, a removable glass front and a door in one of the sides. Both sides had openings for a feeding tray and a water dish and, higher up, a row of ventilation holes that could be closed with a slide, partially or completely. He instilled a thermometer on one of the side walls. The lamps he used had a wattage of 15, 25, and 40, so that he could vary the temperature as necessary.

Since this early design by af Enehjelm, many models followed, which are now available in better pet stores.

The best temperature for the living space in the hospital cage is 104° F (40° C), with as little variation as possible. As soon as the sick bird gets better, the temperature can be dropped gradually. Dissolve an antibiotic in the drinking water (water-soluble Aureomycin, Terramycin, and the like).

One or more hospital cages should be essential equipment for every dedicated aviculturist!

Broken legs: The legs of small exotic finches are generally thin and quite vulnerable. A leg can break easily, especially during a mishap in the catching process. Birds such as mannikins that are frequently troubled by overly long nails, often break one or both legs when they become snagged on something.

Your first response, naturally, is to capture the patient with the utmost care. Then splice the leg with a moderately thick feather shaft (like a chicken feather) or a plastic drinking straw cut lengthwise. Attach the splint with woolen yarn or surgical tape and then make it rigid with collodion, surgical glue, or plaster. Put the patient in a small hospital cage. Cover the floor with a thick layer of sand. Place food and water on the floor, so that the bird can reach it easily. Remove all perches. Provide extra supplements of limestone, cuttle bone, and vitamin D. You can take off the splint after approximately 20 days by dissolving it in acetone (ether is not as good); be extremely careful as the fumes may be harmful to the patient. If the leg hasn't turned black, you can assume that the operation was successful. Be sure to remember that when you wrap a broken leg, you shouldn't do this too tightly. It is advisable to consult an avian veterinarian.

Broken wings: Broken wings are hard to heal. If the bird involved is valuable, go for help to a veterinarian. If you want to try a home treatment, however, cut away the feathers around the break and disinfect the area of the break with antibiotics. Carefully hold the broken parts together and join them with a strong piece of surgical tape. Put the bird in a small cage with its food and drinking bowl on the floor. Remove all perches. Be sure the diet is optimally balanced, and supplement it with vitamins A and D, cuttle bone, low-salt grit, limestone, and green food (spinach). Remove the tape after approximately 20 days.

Bald spots: Feathers can drop out to create bald spots due to vitamin deficiencies, mite infestations, or calcium deficiency. To deal with the problem, make sure the rations are adequate. I suggest you add low-salt grit to the diet. Be sure that there is enough vitamin A, D and B. If there are mites, get a good miticide (ask your pet dealer for advice). Put antibiotics into the drinking water (ask your veterinarian or pet store manager).

Feather picking: Birds sometimes pick the feathers of another bird in more than an occasional way. This can be caused, for example, by boredom, stress, vitamin-, protein-, calcium- and other mineral deficiencies, or overcrowding. The result is bald spots on the victim's body.

First of all, immediately improve the diet drastically; be sure to improve the vitamin and mineral content and add rearing and egg food to the diet, preferably year-round. Add antibiotics (ask your veterinarian) to the drinking water. Combat boredom by adopting the suggestions given under "Egg pecking." If you're overstocked, thin out the collection. Be sure to immediately remove any loose feathers that lie on the floor. If despite your countermeasures the problem persists, a light spray with Bitter Apple® may help. Be sure not to get any spray in the birds' eyes. Whatever you do, don't wait before you take action against feather picking.

Egg pecking: Birds will peck at their own eggs or those of other exotic finches when we don't furnish enough cuttle bone, limestone, grit, and vitamins during the year, but especially during the breeding season. Boredom also can be a cause. Be sure the supplements I just mentioned are in adequate supply, and provide extra vitamin A and D. Counteract boredom by using your imagination in varying the diet. Hang up some jute ropes or, once in awhile, a piece of raw red meat to attract their interest.

Egg binding: Egg binding is the condition where the female can't lay an egg that's ready to be laid. A major cause is breeding a female too young. I warn against this practice at several points in this book for good reason. Never breed female finches younger than 10 to 12 months of age, and don't breed old ones either—not older than five years of age.

Other possible causes include breeding females that have gotten too fat or too weak, or have a serious calcium deficiency. Cold, drafty sleeping quarters could also be a contributing factor. Finally, it is possible that the oviduct isn't developed properly or has become infected. If this last condition is at fault, there is little we can do about it; the only thing we can do is not breed with these females.

To help expel a "stuck" egg, gently dip the lower half of the female's body in alternately cold and lukewarm water. Dab some vegetable oil "under the tail" (in the vent). Put the patient in a hospital cage at 90° F (32° C); when the egg is laid, reduce the temperature slowly to normal. Whatever you do, don't take a chance on breaking the egg inside the bird's body—this could have fatal results. Add antibiotics to the drinking water. If you have to artificially promote laying, be sure not to use the eggs produced this way for breeding. In all cases, it is better to consult an avian veterinarian immediately.

Eye infection: If a bird has an eye problem, for example excessive tearing, place the bird in a darkened cage and treat the infected eye with five percent boric acid ophthalmic ointment (Neosporin® or Neopolycin®), after first rinsing out the eye with lukewarm water or a 0.9 percent saline solution. Add vitamin A and D to the food. Eye infection is often caused by bacteria, so keep perches and housing clean!

Chlorosis: This problem occurs through insufficient nutrition, or improper sanitation. The birds look anything but attractive as their feathers look bedraggled. The beak and legs lose their color. In many cases, small eruptions form on the skin and sometimes on the legs.

The only remedy is a drastic improvement in the food. Provide chickweed, lettuce, endive, and sprouts daily; be sure they are fresh. Add several drops of an antibiotic to the drinking water. Get rid of lice in the bird facility. Eruptions on the skin and legs should be carefully lanced with a disinfected needle. Empty out the pus with sterile cotton or gauze, then cover the affected areas with pure glycerine.

Jaundice: This illness is caused by a deficiency in vitamins or a shortage of food. The skin of the affected birds is yellow, particularly the lower part of the body. The skin can also be quite swollen. Jaundice often follows intestinal catarrh.

Isolate infected birds in a warm spot and provide antibiotics in the drinking water. It helps to provide white bread soaked in milk or water. Make sure the diet is first quality. Provide extra rape seed and a good-quality egg and rearing food. Also offer a daily supply of chickweed, lettuce, or endive. When the birds recover, keep them apart from the rest of the flock until the weather outside is warm and dry.

Rheumatism: This malady is caused by drafts, wet floors, thin perches, and colds. Affected birds suffer considerable pain, practically stop eating and have visibly inflamed ankles.

Remove the affected birds from the collection immediately, and place them in a warm hospital cage. Exposure to a lot of sun is one of the best remedies. If perches are too thin, they naturally have to be replaced (average thickness should be 1½" (4 cm.). Swollen ankles should be treated with a topical application of spirits of camphor. If the swellings start oozing pus, follow the suggestions given under "Swellings." Add antibiotics to the drinking water, and consult an avian veterinarian.

71

Swellings: Swellings typically are a hardening of the upper skin layer and are filled with pus. They can be caused by a variety of irritants, such as insect bites, scrapes, and blood poisoning. Treat swellings with an antiseptic remedy. When the swelling has ripened, lance it carefully and apply antibiotics. Separate the patient in a cage placed in a warm location. For awhile, don't feed seeds; do provide bread soaked in milk, green food, egg- and rearing-food, and for seven days 8 IN 1 "Avilac" for Finches. Provide aftercare for the wounds with some "Stay"™ (Mardel). Consult an avian veterinarian.

Anemia: This problem occurs from time to time if you inbreed too much, particularly with Bengalese and Zebra Finches. The condition can also be brought on by insufficient nutrition, extreme cold, or vermin. The birds appear unattractive, have dull eyes that are sometimes a little inflamed, and the color of beak, legs and skin has faded. The breastbone often protrudes considerably. Affected birds often sleep with their heads buried in the feathers, which tend to be puffed up.

In this case, immediately clear vermin out of the facility. Change and improve the diet. Add vitamin C, low-salt grit, a good grade of finch rearing food, "Avilac," and a lot of greens. Keep the affected birds warm and expose them to sunlight as much as possible. Be sure to furnish fresh bathwater daily (only during the warm hours of the middle of the day) and add a few drops of an antibiotic to the water; this will help return the glow to the feathers.

If you buy medication at the pet store or get some from your veterinarian, be sure to follow the directions precisely. I have known people who have used medication in the exact opposite way as directed on the package. So, take time to read and understand how medication is to be used. Let me add that there are no wonder drugs that can save every bird.

Bronchitis: This infectious disease is caused by colds, sudden, drastic changes in temperature, bath and drinking water that's too cold, or other infections. Affected birds resemble pitiful shaking balls of misery; they gasp, cough now and then, and attempt to shake off the slime that exudes from the beak and/or nostrils.

Immediately separate the stricken birds in a warm spot or hospital cage to avoid infecting the rest of your flock. Thoroughly disinfect the cage or aviary. Consult an avian veterinarian immediately. Add a few drops of antibiotic to the drinking water, including the drinking water for birds that have remained healthy.

Intestinal Infections and Diarrhea: These disturbances can be caused by bacterial infections, coccidia and worms, and therefore are quite contagious. The infection is actually in the intestinal lining. Diarrhea can be caused or worsened by insufficient rations, drinking and bath water that's too cold, egg food or green food furnished too wet, or large changes in temperature.

72

Affected birds are in poor condition, have listless eyes, act sluggish, and have thin, slimy droppings that are generally yellowish-green or white. In many cases, the cloaca (vent) is infected. The thin droppings cause the feathers of the lower body to become dirty and sticky.

Remove oil-rich seed from the diet for two weeks. Separate the sick birds and keep them warm. Furnish extra poppyseed. Add antibiotics to the drinking water. Wash the lower body with lukewarm water, ideally every two days. Add antibiotics to the wash water; further follow the instructions of your avian veterinarian.

Diphtheria: This infectious disease requires immediate remedy! Affected birds pant heavily and cough, have slimy droppings, and inflamed eyes. The nose exudes a slimy moisture that hardens quickly. The birds tend to sit constantly at the drinking fountain to slake their thirst, caused by fever. The most common cause is a cold. Capture the sick birds, and cage them separately in a warm spot. Add antibiotics to the drinking water, and follow the directions of the avian veterinarian.

Take steps to avoid a repeat infection. Examine the aviary carefully to detect openings that promote drafts. Be sure that the diet is correct. Disinfect the aviary and dig and turn the dirt floor good and deep. Incinerate dead birds.

Give sick birds antibiotics once or twice daily, following the advice of your veterinarian. Use a weak solution of boric acid to clean the beak and eyes. Ask your veterinarian how best to protect the rest of your flock. For several months they should get medication in the drinking water.

Tuberculosis: This is one of the most feared and most infectious diseases. The major cause, often, is a cold. Immature birds also can get TB. The sick birds look unattractive, have a rasping respiration that obviously is quite painful, and have slimy droppings tinged with blood. They practically stop eating and become visibly thinner as a result.

Remedies help only if started early. Immediately segregate the sick birds. Administer drops of a strong antibiotic (consult your veterinarian) into the throat, generally twice per day, as directed. Be sure to disinfect the entire bird facility and dig up the soil in unpaved areas. Also put antibiotics in the drinking water, including the water for healthy birds. Burn dead birds immediately!

Constipation: Constipation frequently results from feeding too much egg food, especially if it is too dry. An excess of poppyseed may also cause problems. Other causes can be spoiled or old seed.

Birds with constipation puff up the feathers and stay perched or nervously run up and down. Sometimes it is clear that they can't relieve themselves. The rear of the body may even be swollen. They stop eating and act sluggish. Remedy the problem with green food, a lot of fruit, and rape seed

Red-masked Gouldian cock *(Chloebia gouldiae).*

Photo by author

rubbed with fat. Add antibiotics to the drinking water and vitamins to the food. Above all, be sure that the food you furnish (for example "Avilac" for Finches, during seven days) is top quality and fresh.

Mite Infestation: Red mites (*Dermanyssus avium*) are the worst. This blood-sucking arachnid surfaces from all types of dark hideaways during the evening and night. Favorite hiding places are cracks and seams (especially in nest boxes). In case of heavy infestations, mites may even stay on the birds during the day, so it isn't always good enough merely to transfer affected birds to another, uninfested facility, even if it is thoroughly disinfected. It also doesn't help just to let an infested facility stand empty in hopes of getting rid of red mites; they can live without eating for at least five or six months!

A red mite infestation is easy to notice. The birds are restless at night and peck and scratch continuously. If you shine a flashlight at the birds or their perches, you will be able to see the red parasites easily in most cases. Take good care that you do not personally pick up any mites, because they can cause an irritating, burning eczema in humans; a heavy case can even cause anemia.

Mite infestation can be brought in by wild birds or new purchases and can progress rapidly, since a single female mite can produce approximately 2,600 eggs in its lifetime. So it pays to keep on the alert. During daylight, run a pocketknife through cracks and crevices. If you don't get any blood on it, then there's no trouble. Or else, lay a white cloth in the sleeping coop or on the cage and look for mites on the cloth the next morning.

The moment you confirm a mite infestation, remove all birds from the facility and spray it with a contact insecticide. (Ask your pet store manager to recommend a good product.) Some sprays now on the market can be used without removing birds from the facility. Be sure to spray all holes, crevices, joints, perches, wire mesh, nest boxes, food and water dishes (especially the sides and bottoms) and all other utensils and equipment in the facility. Remove all nesting material and burn it. After letting the insecticide work its benefits for several days, wash everything thoroughly with soapy water. Rinse cages with boiling water. Make sure that your storage areas are also free of mites, otherwise a new infestation will be launched from there. Treat your birds with a powder insecticide or with some commercial brand of spray. Be sure to follow label directions. Under no circumstances should you use Lindane. You can get good results with a 0.15 percent solution of Neguvon.

Use the same remedies for feather lice, feather mites, and shaft mites. These species live on the carotine (protein) of the feather shaft, causing the feathers to drop and general growth and development to be stunted. I can't say enough that absolutely proper sanitation in the bird facility is the only lasting remedy.

Airsac mites: Airsac mite infestation is another simple problem to diagnose. The affected birds have their necks stretched out and have visible problems with swallowing. They appear to sneeze and jerk their heads.

Prevent this problem with a pest strip; in all cases, however, ask your veterinarian for instructions and advice. Don't just hang the strip up; be sure to take off the wrapping and hang it outdoors for 24 hours. Only then hang it, about a yard (1 m.) from the wire mesh—on the outside, so that the birds can't touch it. If you have a single bird in a cage, hang the strip one yard from the cage. With these precautions I have never had bad results with a strip, even though some bird fanciers say they've experienced problems. There are several other products available. Consult your avian veterinarian on this and on proper treatment for the birds.

Airsac mites seldom cause problems in outdoor aviaries. Diamond Sparrows, Gouldian Finches, and Parrot Finches seem to have the most difficulty with airsac mites.

4

Food and Water

___

Seed

EXOTIC FINCHES ARE PRINCIPALLY seed eaters, that is, they feed on all types of grass and weed seeds available in their country of origin. Various types of millet are the main component. Species with small, weak beaks seem to prefer the soft types of millet (like Senegal millet and spray millet). Birds with somewhat stronger bills prefer silver, Morocco and La Plata millet. All types of exotic finches, however, love to snack on spray millet; the seed heads of panicum millet. They also like white seed or, as it is often called, canary grass seed, not to be confused with canary mixture. Further, a good seed mix must contain ripe and unripe grass and weed seed. Many finch species also like niger seed, but this should always be offered in small quantities because of its heavy fat content; excessive consumption can cause liver problems. But since it is rich in minerals, it should not be omitted. Oats (oat groats or hulled) can also be fed, especially in the diet of larger birds (like the Java Sparrow), but it is best to limit it to birds housed in a large aviary. Birds in cramped quarters can grow fat too easily on oats.

Personally I like the following seed mixes:

Gray-headed silverbill cock *Lonchura [odontospiza] caniceps).*

For large finches

canary seed (not canary mixture)		5 oz.
La Plata and red or white millet		1 oz.
oat groats		1½ oz.

75% starch

rape seed	½ oz.
cole seed	½ oz.
niger seed	0.8 oz.
sesame seed	0.3 oz.
linseed	0.3 oz.
hemp seed	0.1 oz.
(if available)	

25% oil bearing

or:

40% canary seed
30% white pearl millet
15% Japanese millet
10% panicum millet
 5% hulled oats

Seed mix for small finches

55% Senegal millet
15% panicum millet
15% white pearl millet
10% canary seed
 3% hulled oats
½% sesame seed
½% poppyseed
½% plantain seed
½% niger seed

Seed treat for all finches

 5% poppyseed (blue)
 5% canary seed
 5% hemp seed (if available)
 5% poppyseed (white)
10% thistle seed
20% niger seed
10% white lettuce seed
20% black lettuce seed
20% sesame seed

Sprouted Seed

Sprouted seed is extremely useful, especially millet, niger seed, grass seed, and weed seed. You may not be able to buy weed seed commercially, but you can gather your own, of course.

To grow sprouts, take a rather thick, smooth towel and wet it with lukewarm water. Spread it out over a tray or flat plate. Sprinkle the seed on it and put it in a humid place. As the sprouting seed bursts open, take it off the

79

Painted Fire Finch *(Emblema picta)*.

towel and rinse it in lukewarm water (a colander would help). Then feed the sprouted seed to the birds in a separate dish.

Don't provide more sprouted seed than the birds can use up in a single day, and if there are leftovers in the evening, take them away. You don't want your birds to eat soured seed, which can cause intestinal upsets.

You can even plant some weed seed on the floor of the aviary. As it sprouts and germinates, the birds will relish it. For this reason, don't remove all the spilled seed from around the feeding dish. The sprouting seed will create a green corner in which the birds will love to root around.

Green Food

There should never be a shortage of green food. This term includes chickweed, collards, leaf and Bibb lettuce, endive, spinach, cabbage, pieces of carrot and carrot tops, celery leaves, broccoli, dandelion, and such. Always provide fresh greens and remove any leftovers around the time that the birds go to roost. Make sure you provide organic greens; if you don't have a sure source, grow it yourself.

Fruit

Many exotic finches love to nibble on pieces of apple, pear, tomato, orange, melon, cherry, grape, grapefruit, berries, raisins and currants (the latter two may also be furnished soaked). If you provide big pieces, hammer a few nails through a board and stick the fruit through the pointed ends. This keeps the fruit clean. Greens and fruit can also be provided in wire baskets sold commercially for this purpose. However, some of the contents will usually fall out.

Food of Animal Origin

Practically all exotic finches like to eat food of animal origin—insects and man-made substitutes, such as universal food, egg food, rearing food, and the like. This type of food becomes a necessity during the breeding season.

In nature, birds also like termites, ant pupae ("ant eggs"), small spiders and similar material. You can provide these to your captive birds as well, plus small mealworms, cut into sections. Better pet stores also sell dried or frozen "ant eggs." You have to prepare dried ant pupae for feeding by first pouring boiling water over them and letting them soak for a half hour. Frozen ant pupae must be thawed for at least three hours.

A good menu should also include moths, fly larvae, and enchytrea (white worms), and you can provide variety by sometimes substituting tubifex, red mosquito larvae, and water fleas (which you can buy in pet stores that sell aquarium supplies). Universal food, rearing food, and egg food are also best bought commercially. If you wish, you can enrich it with finely diced boiled egg and small insects.

Cherry Finch *Aidemoysne [Poephila] modesta).*

Vitamins, Minerals and Trace Elements

Birds living free in their country of origin select from a great variety of insects, seeds and fruits to complete their diet. Away from home in captivity, it is difficult to duplicate all these dietary elements, hard as we may try. One of the most likely deficiencies concerns vitamins. You can buy all types of multivitamins commercially, and these are essential for keeping your birds healthy. Green food and grass- and weed-seed are also extremely important food sources. Furthermore, your birds need to have access to supplements with minerals and trace elements, which are essential for proper plumage and good bone structure and healthy internal organs. You can provide this supplement by furnishing finely ground boiled egg shells, cuttle bone, finely ground oyster shell, enriched limestone and commercial low-salt grit (without charcoal, because some scientists believe that charcoal removes the vitamins A, B_2 and K from the intestinal tract, thus contributing to vitamin deficiency).

Drinking Water and Bath Water

The waterer I like best has a little rock with running water and a small gutter to drain excess water. This setup is rather costly to install and needs to be shut off in winter. Most bird fanciers, therefore, make do with earthenware dishes. This solution isn't very hygienic, because birds will bathe in their drinking water, and dirt and dust can mess up the water. Small water fonts and automatic waterers can also get dirty, but not as badly because they keep providing fresh water. And of course, birds can't bathe in them.

If you use open dishes, cover them with wire mesh. This is especially important in winter in colder climates, as you don't want to run the chance that birds bathe in their drinking dishes and freeze to death.

Check at least every day to make sure the water supply is in order, more often (several times per day) during hot summer weather. Bath water must be replenished several times each day. Bathing dishes can get dirty rather quickly and must absolutely be cleaned regularly.

To give your birds a special treat, dissolve some honey or grape sugar (glucose) in the drinking water several times per week. And now and then, give the finches a small dish of fruit juice. Cover these dishes with a lid made of wire netting, otherwise the birds might bathe in it!

If your water is highly chlorinated, supply rain water instead of tap water. Boil it, cool it for at least three hours, and only then give it to the birds. Spring water, available commercially in various brands, is also excellent!

Feeding Your Finches

Nothing is as important as getting your birds accustomed to a fixed daily routine. Furnish drinking water, bath water, and food at definite times each day, and maintain the same appearance. In other words, if you wear glasses, always wear them. If you wear a hat in winter, wear it in summer, too. Wear a dust coat to protect your clothes and standardize your appearance. If it wears out, try to buy a replacement of the same color. Then keep up this appearance whenever you do any work in the aviary or near your birds.

Feed the birds at a regular time each morning, when they are hungry after a night's rest. Universal food and other soft food can also be furnished at that time of day. This way, it can be consumed as needed and is freely available if any nestlings have to be fed. Also, chances of spoilage are minimized, because you set it out before sunrise or while the sun is still weak. Remember spoilage, and check each evening (again at a regular time) whether any perishable food is left over and throw it away.

Provide seed in open dishes with a lip. Before adding fresh seed, blow away empty hulls. You can get automatic feeders, which should have a glass front so that you can check on the food supply that's left. Check these to see that the flow of seed isn't jammed when the unit is in use and refill as needed.

When you provide fresh bathing and drinking water, wash out the dishes. As you do these chores, softly whistle a tune or talk softly to the birds to keep them calm. A regular routine—regular whistling or humming, regular clothes, regular chore time—will accustom the birds to your presence, and they will not become upset even if you need to look into a nest during the breeding season or when you need to do any chores near them while they are brooding or feeding their young.

Take the opportunity to individually examine birds in your collection to see how they are doing. Pick a time other than the breeding season, or do it when you are moving birds indoors from the garden aviary. Lay the bird on its back in the palm of your hand, and then blow aside some breast- and stomach-feathers. This allows you to inspect the skin. The breast and stomach should have a healthy red color without any yellow discoloration. If you do see some yellow, this generally indicates that the bird has grown too fat because you have been feeding too many oil-rich seeds. Improve the situation by adjusting the diet and by housing the fat birds in a facility where they have more room to exercise.

5

Breeding

NEVER COMMENCE WITH BREEDING too early.
Many species of exotic finches have the capacity to begin breeding as early as
about five months of age. However, if you start them off that young, you will
run into egg binding, weak young, and other troubles. You will be far better
off not to start breeding until your finches are a full year of age.

Preparations

A good-sized breeding cage (about 40″—100 cm.—in length) is required
for effective breeding. (Some species may even require more room.) Keep only
one breeding pair in a cage and provide a choice of nesting places. Your results
will be considerably better, however, using one of the various types of aviaries.
In the first place, the birds have more flying room there, and, secondly, they
can enjoy fresh air and sunlight.

Stick to the general rule that there needs to be at least one cubic yard
(meter) of space per breeding pair. Some pairs seem to prefer an aviary to
themselves for breeding; others show better results if they cohabit with other
pairs, colony style. You will receive specific advice on this topic in the
description of individual species.

Nest Boxes and Nesting Material

Many exotic finches like to build a free-standing nest in the dense foliage
of trees and shrubs. To satisfy this preference, consider providing a variety of

plantings. The seclusion offered by plantings is a definite plus.

The birds will use all types of man-made resting places, however. You can consider nest boxes, baskets, heather, and reeds. The majority of exotic finches prefer the so-called half-open nest box, and others like to breed in a closed nest box with a round entrance hole. Use boxes measuring 6″ cube (15 cm.) for the smaller species. The larger ones should have 7″ cube (18 cm.) or 7″ × 7″ × 8″ (16 × 16 × 20 cm.).

If you use commercial baskets, consider only those with a diameter of about 6″ (15 cm.). Each pair of birds requires at least two nest boxes or baskets, because there should always be a choice.

In the aviary, spread out the nesting equipment as much as possible, in the sleeping coop as well as in the run. Don't hang them close together and do hang them at various heights off the floor. Feel free to supply nest boxes of several types, because a breeding pair from a species generally known to prefer a nest box with a small entry hole may, as individuals, prefer to use a half-open nest box or basket. If you have dense bushes or trees, hang up some wire baskets or canary baskets, half of a coconut shell, and other equipment that the birds can use as foundation for a free-standing nest.

Provide an ample amount of nesting material. Include both dried and fresh-cut grass, coconut fibers, pieces of hemp rope up to 3″ (6 cm.) long, sisal (*Agave sisalana*) fibers, moss, tree bark, leaf veins and whole leaves, (goat) hair, and feathers. Some species also like to use small twigs or needles from conifers. Others like small stones, charcoal, lumps of soil, and peat-moss. For more details, see individual species descriptions.

Mating Behavior

I heartily recommend you take time to observe the mating dance of your exotic finches (using binoculars!). Most species are well worth watching. You will note that generally the male sings a full-throated song, often holding a blade of grass or a twig in his beak. He hops in a circle around the female, beating his tail. Often the mating dance is the only sure way to determine the sex of birds that are not differentiated by color. Several of the Parrot Finches, among others, also like to chase their beloved at amazing rates of speed, especially in a roomy aviary.

After mating, the birds start carrying in all types of building materials. They inspect many nesting sites. The male repeatedly sounds off with his summoning cry, inviting the female to come and inspect sites that he has found. Quite often, the female is not satisfied with the location, so that the male has to go look for a new site for the future nest. You will be able to see that a certain nest box or other location is satisfactory if both birds sit at that site for about 45 minutes. Mating (copulation) often occurs in the nest, but is also possible on a branch or on the ground.

The Nest and the Eggs

Nest construction can be carried out within several days, but may extend surprisingly long (a week or longer). Most birds definitely don't stay with the task constantly; they take breaks regularly to eat, to fly around a little, or to just rest. Many species keep rearranging the nest regularly even if eggs have already been laid. Generally the male brings the building material while the female does the actual construction. Most nests are carefully put together, but I have also encountered large, rough nests with thick walls and long entry tunnels.

It's important you furnish a variety of nest building materials. If you don't, the birds may give up on the job or steal nesting materials from other birds in the aviary. Often the female lays her first eggs before the nest is completely finished.

The first egg can be expected three to five days after mating. The female will continue laying one egg a day until the clutch is complete. It can vary between two and nine eggs, but usually will range from four to six eggs. After the third or fourth egg is laid, brooding begins. The clutch is brooded for 11 to 16 days, and the young hatch after about two weeks.

Brooding

While brooding takes place, give your birds complete quiet. Interruptions of any king can cause the parents to abandon the eggs or the young. For this reason, I suggest you don't make close-up inspections of the nest. You should be able to tell by the actions of the parents whether everything is going right. Some birds are more tolerant of nest inspections, although this doesn't mean that it is wise to actually make these inspections. The tolerant species include Zebra Finches, Bengalese, and Long-tailed Grass Finches. During breeding, you need to maintain a temperature between 65° and 80° F (18° and 28° C), and a humidity between 60 and 80 percent, depending on the species.

The Young

For the first seven to 10 days after hatching, the young birds are kept warm day and night. That's understandable, realizing that most hatchlings come out of the egg naked, or with just a little down. The young of many species very quickly start their begging cries; others are very quiet, especially for the first three days. At a week to 10 days, the first feathers break through and the eyes open. From then on, the young develop rapidly, and they leave the nest box or basket after about 21 days.

The parents feed the young regularly, provided the right food is available. Unlike the practice of other birds, the parents of finches often won't remove droppings from the nest. Rather, the young themselves, once they are about four days old, make the proper movements to deposit droppings on the edge

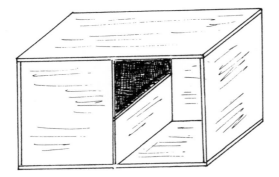

Breeding box for Australian grass finches.

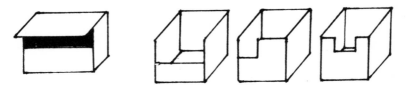

Variations in finch breeding boxes.

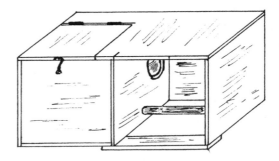

Breeding box for *Estrildid* species.

of the nest, where they dry up quickly. This way the droppings won't pose the danger of infections.

Once the young fly out, they will spend a lot of time on the ground the first few days. Toward evening, however, most of them will get back into the parental nest to sleep. There are species, to be sure, where the young do not spend the night in the nest but stay outside or in a dark, wind-free spot in the aviary. As mentioned earlier, it is therefore very important to maintain the right temperature. So be sure that if there are young birds in an outdoor aviary, that they spend the night in the warm sleeping coop (night shelter).

After one to three weeks, if all goes well, the young become independent and will be fed by the parents only rarely. In many species, young should be removed from the parents at that stage, because otherwise the male will start to chase them around. This prevents the parents from starting a new breeding cycle. However, in cases where the parents like to have their young around, don't hesitate to leave them together; that way the young learn about life from their parents.

Leg Banding

Even though you want to disturb breeding birds as little as possible, you will have to take the young in hand at least once, namely to band them. Many bird societies require young birds entered into shows to be banded with a closed ring. These types of leg bands can be purchased directly from the various bird societies. The ring will be marked with information such as your personal identification code, the individual bird's number and the year of the bird's hatch. This gives you clear evidence that a certain bird comes from your aviary. Many bird fanciers prefer an open, plastic, colored band to identify their finches (placed on birds after weaning), allowing the fancier to avoid the risk of undesirable side effects from taking the young out of the nest to band them. Problems that could occur include the parents' refusal to come back to the nest, to feed the young or throwing the banded young out of the nest. Many bird parents take fright when they encounter their young in the nest with a shiny band. Because they endeavor to keep the nest clean the first few days, they regard the band as a foreign object and try to remove it. The fact that a young bird is attached to the band seems to be of no significance to the cleaning bird!

Exotic finches are best banded at eight days of age. Blacken the ring in a candle flame before banding.

Not everyone has the knack for proper banding. Observe the process at the hands of an experienced bird fancier. Start the process at the onset of dusk when the female has become less intent on keeping the nest clean. That way you can almost surely avoid the young being thrown out of the nest. In any case, it pays to check every morning for a couple of days whether "everyone is still there."

The proper steps are as follows. Rub a little petroleum jelly on the leg and "glue" the first three toes together. "Glue" the small rear toe against the leg. This creates a straight line, so to speak. Now slide the band over the toes and the ball of the foot onto the leg. Then use a pointed match to flip the small toe carefully from under the band. Clean leg and toes thoroughly with a cotton ball, position the band correctly around the chick's leg, and the banding operation is complete.

Use a small band (with a diameter of 2 millimeters) for small species, such as Orange-cheeked Waxbills, Strawberry Finches, and African Golden-breasted Waxbills. Use a medium-sized band (of 2.3 millimeters) for birds the size of Silverbills, Melba Finches, and Lavender Waxbills. Use a little larger size band (2.5 millimeters) for birds the size of Spice Finches, Gouldian Finches, Cut-throat Finches, Parrot Finches, Zebra Finches, and Diamond Sparrows. If you use bands that are too large for the bird, you run the chance of losing the bands sooner or later. The National Finch Society carries sizes for all finches and softbills.

First Molt

Once the young are one or two weeks old, they acquire their colored beaks. Earlier their beaks are black, or yellow in the case of some Parrot Finches. At six weeks of age the first, juvenile molt begins; it can last from one to two months, depending on the species. First the small stomach feathers and the feathers on the abdomen acquire their definitive form and color; followed by breast-, rump- and upper tail-feathers, back and flanks—in that order. Finally, the wing-, head-, and tail-feathers.

During molting, your birds require special care. Provide the proper temperature, sunlight, and a well-balanced diet. A sudden change in temperature can cause the molt to be interrupted, which in turn can cause the birds to become sick, and even die. The diet absolutely must include oyster shell, vitamin-enriched limestone, ground shells, cuttle bone, sprouted seed, green food, yeast and vitamins. Another absolute must is exposure to direct sunlight; if that's impossible, use a fluorescent bulb. Do not use a sunlamp, however, as these are injurious to birds' eyes. Switch the heat lamp on for limited time periods only, perhaps three to 15 minutes a day, starting with three minutes and gradually working up to the maximum. Place the lamp so the bird can also sit out of its glow, should it so desire.

Artificial lighting is also recommended, especially if new birds arrive during the fall or winter. The whole idea is to provide them with daylight as long as possible, allowing them more time to eat and get used to their environment, not to mention captivity itself. Do not, however, place the cage directly in the sunlight; although finches like warmth and sun, they also need to have shade. (On the other hand, it is not sensible to place the cage in a location where no sunlight comes in at all.)

Crossbreeding

The Australian grass finches are extremely well suited for crossbreeding. Many crosses occur spontaneously. Crossbreeding, however, entails a sizable risk, namely to the racial purity of bird species, especially so when you cross species that resemble each other closely. Purposeful crossbreeding is often quite difficult, but I won't go into details in this book, since this is really a separate branch of the bird fancy. Personally, I attach much greater value to the breeding of pure species, especially with an eye on the possibility that within a short time importing many tropical birds will be severely restricted. Since this eventuality has not yet occurred, every serious bird fancier should cooperate in the breeding of as many pure avian species as possible, so that the hobby can continue into the future. To this I add that most crossbred birds are sterile and therefore cannot be used for further breeding. So it is best to concentrate our efforts on the breeding and care of pure species.

Use of Foster Parents

It is generally known that Society Finches often serve as foster parents for other exotic finches. Nevertheless, you should do all you can to motivate the birds in your collection to do their own brooding. Nothing excels brooding with natural parents. I am strongly opposed to the practice of consistently employing foster parents for raising birds of high commercial value, like Gouldian Finches, for example. Going about the business in this way has—I feel—no place in hobby breeding. The inevitable result is that the females of valuable finches are sooner or later converted into egg-laying machines; obviously this practice comes a cropper and the "mechanized" female dies from egg binding. It doesn't work either to first use females to produce many eggs and then later to let them brood and raise a set of young on their own. Even if they do raise these young successfully, they are usually weak of constitution.

It has also been proven beyond a doubt that species that have been raised generation after generation by foster parents lose much of their own brooding instinct. In other words, they are barely able to raise a generation of young on their own. The first symptoms are incomplete nest building, egg pecking, and poor sexual drive.

If you provide proper housing and diet, you will be able to breed all the finch species named in this book. You will have to work, and work hard, for this goal. Some species are easier to breed than others, but they will give you good results with some extra attention.

Still, occasions may arise that give you no choice but to make use of foster parents. At that point, you will have to weigh the advantages of foster parenting against the risks outlined above. Consider whether you are willing to lose a few eggs or young to promote nature's plan. Don't forget that young raised by foster parents generally adopt the behavior of their foster parents,

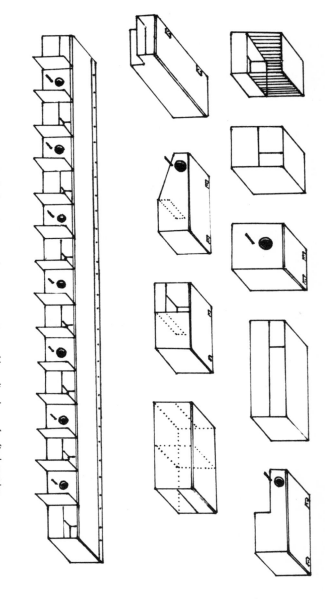

Depending on individual requirements, there are many types of breeding boxes for finch species.

Angola Cordoin Bleu hen *(Uraeginthus angolensis).* *Photo by author*

The Longtailed Grass Finch *(Poephila acuticauda)* makes an ideal aviary bird; it is peaceful and hardy and breeds readily. *Photo by author*

including song, mating dance, search for nesting sites, and choice of building materials.

Prof. Dr. Karl Immelmann and others have conducted experiments showing that behavior is literally imprinted on Zebra Finch young in the first 50 days of their life. If Zebra Finch eggs are brooded by Bengalese who continue to care for the hatchlings, the young Zebra Finches receive the imprint of the Bengalese. Naturally this will lead to great difficulties later on, when the foster young start breeding their own. This problem is even greater if the foster young are paired with birds raised naturally, in order to prevent, for example, inbreeding. Both partners will have had a different education! Immelmann demonstrated that a "mistaken" imprinting could be corrected up to the 50th day of life, provided that the young Zebra Finches are kept exclusively with members of their own species, without having any Bengalese within sight or hearing. As far as we now know, imprinting works this way for all exotic finches. Once it is acquired, whether from natural parents or from foster parents, it is a determining factor for life. Nonetheless, we should do everything possible to try to change the imprinting of foster young to the proper type for their species.

To do this effectively, remove foster young from their foster parents as soon as they can eat on their own, and put them with birds of their own species. If you can manage this within 50 days of hatch, the chances are good that a proper imprinting will be achieved. Young that stay with foster parents beyond the 50th day of life are not likely later to exhibit much interest in others of their own species. Rather, they will be attracted only to the species of their foster parents. If you plan to breed with foster young, you will avoid difficulties by mating individuals raised by the same species of foster parent (but avoid inbreeding). African Silverbills and, to a lesser extent, Zebra Finches also can be used as foster parents.

Even though Bengalese are favorite foster parents, you need to know certain points to succeed with them. You can't just shove eggs or young underneath them and expect to succeed.

Say that you have eggs from a clutch that has been abandoned and you also have a pair of Bengalese that are brooding. The first step is to remove the eggs from the Bengalese and distribute them to other brooding Bengalese. Make sure that the clutches involved are not too far apart in the length of time they have been brooded. Then take the abandoned eggs to the Bengalese nest that has been emptied. If you have young that have been abandoned for some reason by the natural parents, you can transfer them to Bengalese only if these have young of about the same age. Again, you will have to distribute the young of the adoptive parents among the nests of other Bengalese.

If you have experience with Bengalese you will know that two birds of the same sex, two males for example, can function as a pair. They build a nest together and will brood imaginary eggs. This type of odd couple can also function as foster parents—very ably, in fact—especially if you provide them with some infertile or stone eggs while they act as a brooding pair. This stimulates their brooding behavior so that you can then bring young from other exotic finches to them for foster care. Once the young hatch, it can happen that the natural parents will help feed them, provided they are housed in the same facility. They will be attracted by the begging cries of the young, and to have them share in their care can only promote proper imprinting.

Granatina granatina.

6

The Finch Species

Genus *Aegintha* (Red-browed Finches)

Sydney Waxbill *Aegintha temporalis*

DESCRIPTION: Gray crown; lores and eyebrows much broader in male than female. Rump and part of the back red; nape light beige. Ear-coverts brownish gray; the underside is also gray. Wings, shoulders and neck yellow (less in the female); back brown, tail black. Often, the underside has a deep red reflection. Eyes dark brown; beak red; legs yellowish-brown. Length: four inches (10 cm).

DISTRIBUTION AND HABITAT: From Cape York in East Australia to the southeastern coast of South Australia; also on Kangaroo Island (below Adelaide). It occurs along the edges of forests, in parks, in large gardens and along the banks of rivers and lakes.

CAPTIVITY: This species is a slender and quick little bird; it does best in a good-sized aviary with a rich planting. The species does not do too well in cages and indoor vitrines. Nevertheless, the Sydney Waxbill is extremely sensitive to cold, so if you have this species be sure the temperature is never allowed to drop below 65° F (18° C). It is also sensitive to high humidity, so it is best housed in roomy indoor aviaries. Males as well as females share in nest-building, although the female concentrates more on the nest cup. Generally they like a half-open or enclosed nest box—especially the "coconut-type." It does happen repeatedly that they build a free bottle-shaped nest in the bushes. They will use building materials of dry grass, hair, moss, wool, coconut fibers, small feathers, and the like. When the nest is completed, the female starts laying quite soon, provided that she is undisturbed. Both males and females are extremely sensitive to disturbances, and if they occur, the birds usually abandon the nest, even if they already have eggs or young. Under favorable conditions, the female lays three or four eggs, which are brooded 13-14 days.

The male has interesting, clear, and somewhat monotonous but still appealing whistles that he utters before mating. He also has amusing dance steps during his mating dance, which he performs with the tail atilt. The entire performance is extremely rewarding to watch.

Only Japan continues to be a source of these birds, and many times they are not available. Australia has had an export ban in effect since the early 1960s. As a consequence, we must treat the birds now in this country with the utmost care, especially since it has not been possible to keep these birds alive more than three years, at least until now.

FOOD: See STAR FINCH and ZEBRA FINCH.

OTHER NAMES: Red-headed or Red-browed Finch.

Genus *Aidemosyne* (Cherry Finches)

Cherry Finch *Aidemosyne modesta*

DESCRIPTION: Crown dark red-brown; nape and back chocolate brown; rump lighter, often with off-white, poorly formed wavy designs. Primaries brown with white edges. Eyebrow white with black wavy design. Tail black with white spots on the outer feathers. Underparts white with small brown bars. The female lacks the dark spot below the beak. The outermost primaries are black in the male and gray in the female. Eyes dark brown, beak black, legs brownish pink. Length: four inches (11 cm.).

DISTRIBUTION AND HABITAT: From Townsville in Queensland to the central region of New South Wales and to the border of Victoria (Australia); in gardens, shrubs, grassland, near water. Outside the breeding season in large groups, often together with Bicheno's Finches, but always near water.

CAPTIVITY: This bird has become popular in recent years and is rather expensive; yet it is worth the money from the viewpoint of its color and its behavior. Acclimatization can cause difficulties; only experienced hobbyists should give these birds a try. They build a round nest, often in bushes, but also in canary nest boxes and the like. Rubner has written that females can be distinguished from males only by means of a clear-white lore, about 5 millimeters in width, which runs from the beak above the eyes; males lack the lores.

The female lays four to six white eggs which are brooded by both partners; they hatch in 12 days. Absolute quiet is a prime requirement. To avoid brooding problems, let Bengalese or African Silverbills brood the eggs. Personally, I prefer the latter as foster parents because they are relatives of this species. In fact, the two species have frequently been crossed.

Breeding Cherry Finches in the colder or even milder states is best done indoors. The birds like heat and don't do well in temperatures below 65° F (18° C). They should have ample plantings, because they tend to be shy, particularly during the breeding season. Although they are nervous about outside disturbances, they tolerate other finches quite well. It is important to keep these finches in pairs, because as singletons they pine away. In order to obtain good breeding pairs, give the species the opportunity to choose their own partners. As soon as the nest is completed, remove all building materials (the same applies when they use a nest box). The young leave the nest when they are about 21 days old.

FOOD: Ripe and half-ripe seeds, sprouted millet, small berries, greens, and a variety of live food and rearing food.

OTHER NAMES: Modest Grass Finch and Plum-headed Finch: sometimes Plum-capped Finch.

Genus *Amadina* (Cut-throat Finches)

Cut-throat Finch *Amadina fasciata*

DESCRIPTION: Light fawn; each feather is marked with a small black edge; underside chocolate; tail gray, throat whitish, with pronounced red stripe across. The hen lacks the red throat band and the chocolate abdomen. Eyes brown, beak and legs are a light flesh color. Length: five inches (12 cm.).

DISTRIBUTION AND HABITAT: South of the Sahara in both West and East Africa, down to the far south of Tanzania in the east. Also in Mozambique, Zimbabwe (Rhodesia), Botswana and Transvaal. The species lives in the lowlands and along the forest edge but is also found on savannas, in parks and gardens. They build their nests in low bushes or trees; they also will use abandoned and even current weaver nests.

CAPTIVITY: This bird is commonly kept by novice as well as experienced fanciers. The finch is easy to acquire, relatively inexpensive, and uncomplicated to keep in a roomy cage as well as in an aviary. In either facility, it can be brought to breed easily. Do be sure to provide this bird a steady supply of minerals and cuttle bone, since the female is rather susceptible to egg binding. In general, however, the Cut-throat Finch has a strong constitution. It has a soft, trilling song, performed with puffed-up neck and throat feathers, and often performs its summoning call, "chirp, chirp."

During the breeding season these finches, unfortunately, tend to pester other breeding pairs. They visit their nests, causing a certain disquiet that may lead other birds to abandon their nests. Cut-throat Finches have been known to steal building materials from other birds, which causes a great deal of consternation among those that already are brooding eggs or raising young.

The female lays four to seven eggs, which she broods with the aid of the male for about 12-14 days. There are occasions where the female produces extra large clutches. I have seen a nest with eight eggs, and Aschenborn reports one with nine eggs. If you encounter such large clutches, it is best to take a few eggs away.

During brooding, the birds need absolute quiet. I say this with emphasis, because if disturbed, they will abandon eggs or young sooner or later. After about a month, the young leave the nest and then are fed, mainly by the male, for only a short while. The young look a lot like the female at the start, although sometimes a little red or brown can be distinguished in immature males.

Carl Aschenborn cites an observation by Karl Neunzig, which you can easily observe for yourself: in captivity, young males leave the protection of the nest only when they can be readily distinguished from the females by their first brown chest spots and red throat stripe. These are, of course, not as clearly visible as in mature adult males.

You will be able to get three to four sets of young from a breeding pair, so that 20 or more young in one year are not unusual. Dr. Karl Rusz cites a champion breeding pair that raised 176 young in three years without any break. I definitely don't recommend, however, that you try to achieve a record of this type. I mention this piece of information mainly to inform you without any intention to motivate you to duplicate it.

Cut-throat Finches are relatively cold-tolerant, once they have been acclimatized. However, they should always be kept in a separate cage or aviary. Females should be at least nine months of age before they are started into breeding. For nesting material furnish dry grass, plant fibers (agave), strips of bark, small feathers and coconut fibers.

FOOD: All varieties of millet, canary seed, and similar seeds; also sprouted seeds, spray millet, green feed, half-ripe grass and weed seed. Provide small, cut-up mealworms, white worms, maggots, rearing and egg food and other protein sources all year round, but especially during the breeding season. Some birds like fruit (apple, pear, berries), but a wide variety of greens is of the first importance! To prevent egg binding supply the females with codliver oil and various vitamins.

Red-headed Finch   *Amadina erythrocep'hala*

DESCRIPTION: Somewhat resembles the Cut-throat finch, but the male's entire head is crimson; the collar is missing. The female has a gray-brown head, and the underside is less intense. Young males can be differentiated from the females by the red head. Eyes brown, beak and legs flesh-colored. Length: five inches (13 cm.).

DISTRIBUTION AND HABITAT: From South Africa northward to Angola and Natal; in dry open savannas in pairs or small flocks. They build their own nests only by exception; they prefer to move into an abandoned weaver nest, or to evict brooding weavers from their abode. They also build their nests in buildings, like the House Sparrow (*Passer domesticus*); colony breeder.

CAPTIVITY: This species has become commonplace in aviaries in Europe, not alone because it breeds well. Like the Cut-throat Finch, the Red-headed Finch is not a good candidate for the group aviary because it has the undesirable habit of visiting and destroying the nests of other birds, including those of its own kind! It is best to house a single pair in a separate, roomy aviary, breeding cage or vitrine, with good plantings, so the birds can brood successfully and in peace! The female is quite sensitive to disturbances, even relatively minor ones. You can't afford to check on eggs or young, even with the utmost care!

Breeding pairs prefer a half-open nest box (like Cut-throat Finches), but I have often noticed that they will take over and remodel nests of other exotic finches. You don't have to worry about this species as far as staying healthy and raising young are concerned, as long as you provide good food. A breeding pair may even build a free-standing nest, which is roomy, almost

Genus *Amandava* (Avadavats)

African Golden-breasted Waxbill   *Amandava subflava*

DESCRIPTION: Olive-brown above; bright yellow below. Red rump; orange breast. Red streak through the eyes. Eyes brown, beak coral red, legs brown. The female is much duller in coloration. Length: three and a half inches (9 cm.).

DISTRIBUTION AND HABITAT: From Senegal to Ethiopia and further south to eastern South Africa, except for southwestern Africa and the Congo Valley. The birds keep to the ground a lot and the nest is constructed close to the ground in a grass clump or in a small, dense bush. They will also take over nests of other finches, which they renovate somewhat and adapt to their own needs. After the breeding season, they can be encountered in large flocks, especially in grass and along waterways.

CAPTIVITY: This easy-to-keep bird has the qualities of rich color, a loving disposition, and good breeding success. Ornithologists recognize a number of subspecies. The subspecies differ only slightly and get mixed up in the bird trade. This is a real pity. I wish dealers would distinguish between the small differences in color and shape, because this would be a plus for specialized bird fanciers.

The most commonly sold species comes from West Africa and is named *Amandava subflava.* A few of the less common species are the northeastern form, called *Amandava s. subflava,* which also is sporadically found in the West; and the form *Amandava s. clarkei,* which is found in East Africa and without shape and often with a small entry way. It's worth noting that young males do not leave the nest until they have achieved their distinctive red head pattern, similar to the situation with Cut-throat Finches. Red-headed Finches will breed only if they have been acclimatized at a favorable temperature, 60° F (20° C). In my experience, the best breeding results are achieved in a roomy box cage.

The hen usually lays three to six eggs. Incubation time: 12-13 days. Both sexes set on the eggs; during the day the male sets longer than the female; during the night both parents are on the nest, although the male sometimes sleeps in another nest, or close by on a branch. After 23-24 days the young will leave the nest. They are able to reproduce after six months, but breeding should be restricted until the birds are at least one year old. This species has hybridized with the Cut-throat Finch, and the hybrids are fertile.

FEED: Furnish a good seed mix, and for variety, ripe and half-ripe grass and weed seed. Supplement with insects, rearing- and egg-food, small cut-up mealworms, white worms, maggots, ant pupae, lots of greens, cuttle bone, vitamins and minerals.

Amandava formosa.

Amandava subflava.

103

South Africa. This last-named subspecies is less sturdy than the other two. But any of them can be brought to breed successfully, provided that they are well acclimatized. That means that newly arrived birds should be placed in quarantine for at least 30 days and then gradually acclimatized to the local outside temperature. The bird must spend the winter in warm conditions (around 65° F; 18° C).

In most cases, the species will move into a closed nest box, but at times a pair will build a nest in bushes. At first view, the nest looks quite ramshackle, but despite its rough, unattractive appearance and construction, the nest is absolutely safe. A free nest is round and enclosed, with a small, narrow entry way. Eggs are laid in clutches of three or four, and are brooded by the female as well as the male. The young hatch after 11 days, or perhaps 12-13 days in colder weather. While parents feed the young, be sure they have a good quality rearing- and/or egg-food available as well as a variety of small insects and sprouted seed. They also should get fresh greens, especially sprouted niger seed.

When the young have become independent, remove them from the parents to stimulate the female into starting a new clutch. The Golden-breasted Finches are usually pleasant toward other species, but during the breeding season they may be somewhat quarrelsome with other birds. If the aviary is not too densely populated, and there is enough plant life to provide hiding places for those birds that want it, there should be no difficulty. The species sing without interruption their not unattractive song. They are continually cheerful and friendly, and they treat each other pleasantly; they do especially well in cages and vitrines.

FOOD: Furnish all types of small millet, spray millet, and panicum millet in particular. Grass and weed seed are also of the first importance; so is animal protein, which is particularly essential (see the remarks on this topic under RED-EARED WAXBILL).

Green Avadavat   *Amandava formosa* (sometimes *Stictospiza formosa*)

DESCRIPTION: Upperparts olive-green with a golden sheen on the rump and uppertail coverts. Tail black. Underparts greenish-yellow, with dark green and white bars on the sides. The female is duller, with a grayish hue on the underparts and face. Eyes brown, beak red, legs pinkish. Young birds still have a black beak and lack the design on the flanks. Length: four inches (10 cm.).

DISTRIBUTION AND HABITAT: Central India. The bird occurs in grassland, cultivations and cane fields, where it also builds its nest. During the breeding season, it lives in pairs, at other times in small groups.

CAPTIVITY: This bird is now frequently offered in the trade, in part because of its friendly disposition and attractive colors. I have consistently found it a quiet aviary bird that doesn't have complicated demands and that breeds well, provided it is properly cared for. It doesn't cause any problems for other birds during the breeding season. In a group aviary, it doesn't associate much with other birds but tends to stay on the floor, under bushes and in grass clumps. In the winter, it requires a lightly heated facility. In the wild, they build a large, round nest in cane fields or long grass tussocks, but in captivity they seldom get to building a free nest. They like half-open nest boxes in a well-planted aviary.

Don't disturb the birds during the breeding process. The female especially is quite nervous and will leave the nest at the least disturbance. She will, however, return once everything has become peaceful and safe again; this nervousness is one reason why the Green Avadavat is not very suited to life as a cage bird.

Recently imported birds must be first housed in a warm, roomy indoor aviary (70° F; 22° C); after approximately six weeks they can be placed in a well-planted outdoor aviary. During the fall and winter, they must be housed indoors again. The female usually lays four or five eggs. The species will certainly come to breed if their aviary offers the necessary privacy.

FOOD: Provide ample animal protein, especially during the breeding season. For additional advice, see the next section on the RED AVADAVAT.

Red Avadavat *Amandava amandava*

DESCRIPTION: Fiery red; back and wings are a light reddish brown. Rump red, tail black. Lore and border of the eye are black. There are clear white spots on the neck, along the flanks, and on the rump. The tips of the primaries are also white. After the fall molt, the feathers are an even brown because the new feathers have brown edges that wear off only in late winter. This may give the impression that a new molt is taking place, but this is not the case. The female has a dirty yellow underside. The rump is yellowish-orange; the upperside is greenish-gray. The wings are dark greenish-brown. The white dots are noticeably fewer, and occur only along the flank, on the end of the primaries and wing coverts. Eyes and beak are red, the legs grayish-brown. The young closely resemble the female, but they still have a black beak. Length: four inches (10 cm.).

DISTRIBUTION AND HABITAT: India, Pakistan, South Nepal, Southeast Asia (except Malaya), and Indonesia (Java and the Lesser Sundas; introduced in Sumatra, Singapore, Mauritius, Réunion, Fiji and many other places). The bird occurs in grass and reeds, in fields and meadows, and even in parks and gardens. It builds nests in clumps of grass, in dense, low bushes, and even on the ground, well hidden among vegetation. The *Amandava a. flavidiventris* comes from Indo-china.

CAPTIVITY: The species is quite popular, in part because of its colorful appearance. Beginning fanciers can expect good results with these birds, including active breeding. General care, especially during breeding, requires one's full attention, of course. Beginners probably do well because the species has been bred in captivity for many years. Especially in a densely planted aviary, birds raise two (even three) sets of young. I have had the best success in a small aviary, where I housed only one pair of Red Avadavats. As soon as the nest was complete and there were young in the nest, I gave the parents freedom to fly free in the garden (unfortunately, this is illegal in the United States). In the garden they went hunting for small insects and the like among the leaves and in the ivy. Still, I made sure that they could find all types of protein food, such as ant pupae and white worms, within the aviary. I also provided mosquito larvae, spiders, water fleas (daphnia), all types of seed (especially panicum millet), greens, sprouted seeds, grass and weed seeds and fruit. Just prior to the time that the young were ready to leave the nest, I closed the aviary again to avoid the risk that parents and young would escape. Both sexes have an attractive song. The female doesn't trill as loudly as the male. The mating dance is also interesting. The male goes about with a stretched out head and a drooping, spread tail.

The Red Avadavat (Tiger Finch) is more likely to build a free nest than the Green Avadavat; it does so in a bush or in ivy. It also uses half-open nest boxes. The free nest is keg-shaped or bag-shaped, with one or two entry ways of about four inches (10 cm.). Generally, the female lays four to six eggs. If you find clutches of six or more eggs, you may be dealing with two females. Several eggs from a large clutch belonging to a true pair may be infertile.

Provide a quiet environment for breeding birds. They are nervous breeders that can quickly decide to leave the nest to start again elsewhere. Don't house them in an overly large collection. The male defends the nest aggressively, and when he considers the nest to be endangered (often by other birds in the near vicinity), the breeding pair will get so upset that nothing much will come from their breeding.

When you buy Tiger Finches, be especially sure that you are getting a true pair. Outside of the breeding season, the male is not easy to distinguish from the female, but in breeding color, the male attains a beautiful red color with white dots. Outside of the breeding season, you can find all kinds of gradations between the normal, "off-color" and the "fancy" in-season red color, hence few males resemble each other. Many have large amounts of yellow, and others have red or brown. A number of dealers have taken advantage of the situation and have artificially colored their birds red, green, purple, and other colors. They give these "counterfeit" birds all sorts of fancy sounding names and charge high prices. Recent federal laws ban these from the United States.

There is a subspecies with a yellow belly, *Amandava amandava flavidiventris,* which occasionally is available in the trade. Once, in 1966, I had the opportunity to work with a pair of these birds, and I found that the behavior and breeding habits are almost identical to those of the nominate form. The subspecies can justifiably be called Yellow-belly Tiger Finch. Both species prefer to breed in an aviary planted with clumps of grass, dense bushes and ivy, where they have the opportunity to build a free nest. In good weather, there is no reason to avoid keeping either species in an outside aviary, but in the winter months they should be kept in a lightly heated facility, at about 65° F (18° C). They are peaceable toward others of their genus and other small finches as well. With good care, they can get quite old; there are known cases of birds achieving eight to even 15 years of age.

FOOD: I made reference to good feeding practices earlier in this section. Further, be sure not to overfeed vitamins and cuttle bone to avoid egg binding, to which the female is rather susceptible. For further suggestions, see the section on the AFRICAN GOLDEN-BREASTED WAXBILL.

OTHER NAME: Tiger Finch, Strawberry Finch.

Genus *Bathilda* (Star Finches)

Star Finch   *Bathilda [Neochmia] ruficauda*

DESCRIPTION: Face red, as are crown and throat; the back of the head, the neck and shoulders are grass green with a blue reflection. Rump rose-red with a whitish rose-red scalloped design. Wings grass green with light edges; pin feathers of the wings darker green. Tail black-red; breast and flanks yellow-green. Belly yellow to whitish-yellow. Face, breast and flanks are richly covered with white dots. Eyes red, beak dark red, legs yellowish. Length four inches (10 cm.). Two subspecies.

DISTRIBUTION AND HABITAT: Northern Australia, down to the Ashburton River on the west and northern New South Wales in the east (Cayley); always near water in tall grass, rice and sugar-cane fields, bushes and trees; often together with Crimson Finches.

CAPTIVITY: This species is quite popular. The female is not easy to distinguish from the male, but with experience, sexing can be done quickly because the red on the throat of the female is less intense. Cheeks and forehead are not as intensely red. Star Finches are easy to breed, provided they are kept in a well-planted, quiet aviary. For planting, select tall grass, reeds, ivy, and dense bushes. The birds are exceptionally friendly to fellow inhabitants. In roomy outside aviaries, they usually will build a free nest in a little bush. Don't disturb them there, as they are quite sensitive. With any luck, you will be able to count on three clutches per season. The clutches consist of three to five eggs, which are brooded 13 days. The young leave the nest after 22 to 25 days. During fall and winter Star Finches must be housed indoors at room temperature.

Bathilda ruficauda.

A Star Finch cock (left) with two immature sons. Like many species, coloring in the young birds more closely resembles that of the hen.
Photo by A. Sloots

FOOD: During the breeding season, a rich variety of insects, seeds, greens, and commercial egg and rearing food must be available; the birds tend to throw their young from the nest when the food is not to their liking.

Genus *Chloebia* (Gouldian Finches)

Gouldian Finch *Chloebia gouldiae*

DESCRIPTION: Scarlet head, bordered with a narrow black band, followed by a broad turquoise-blue band. Throat and chin black. Breast deep purple, followed by golden-yellow. Neck, wings, and tail green. Undertail coverts white. Black tail. Middle tail feathers like needle points. Eyes brown, beak white with a red tip, legs pinkish. The female is duller and her bill becomes dark gray during the breeding season. In addition to the red-headed form, there is a black-headed form (most common in the wild) and a yellow-headed form (quite rare). Length: five inches (14 cm.).

DISTRIBUTION AND HABITAT: Generally the birds spread over the tropical part of North Australia, from Derby eastward to the Gulf of Carpentria and to Charters Towers. Especially the Kimberley district is rich in these birds. They move around a great deal, so an exact range is hard to describe. They live on the grassy plains, often near watercourses; also in mangrove swamps and thickets.

CAPTIVITY: This bird is the keystone of every serious collection. They are easy to acquire, in part because of heavy importation from Europe and Japan. A single pair can be brought to breeding in a roomy cage, but they prefer garden or (especially) indoor aviaries. In an aviary, several pairs can be housed together; the minimum is three, the maximum is five. Gouldian Finches are pleasant toward other birds, and there is no reason not to house them with other Australian finches. They need nest boxes of at least 6″ × 6″ × 10″ (15 × 15 × 25 cm.), with an entry hole two inches (5 cm.) in diameter. For nesting material, they use either dry or fresh grass and hay, leaf veins, sisal rope and coconut fibers. Don't furnish material in lengths greater than four inches (10 cm.), to avoid birds entangling themselves. Supply ample amounts, because some birds like to build a large-sized nest. Clutches produced in captivity consist of three to eight eggs (usually five or six), which are brooded by both parents for about 14 days. The new generation leaves the nest at 21 to 24 days of age. The first molt occurs at eight to ten weeks; at five months, the young show adult colors.

Remember that the birds can't take low temperatures. The best breeding results occur at temperatures above 77° F (25° C). To achieve a good molt, the temperature should never drop below 72° F (22° C). Sick birds should be isolated and kept at a temperature of at least 77° F (25° C), and in my experience a constant 86° F (30° C) is best. During molt, birds are very sensitive to temperature changes and will even stop the molt if temperatures drop below 70° F (21° C). Humidity also is extremely important; at a temperature of 77° F (25° C), the humidity should be kept at 70 percent. You should have a good thermometer and hygrometer to monitor the environment. Some pairs are prolific breeders, but for others Bengalese must be used as foster parents.

FOOD: Provide all types of small millet, especially Senegal, Japanese, panicum and silver millet. They will eat some canary grass seed and a little niger seed daily. Also provide a large variety of insects, egg and rearing food, sprouted millet, prostrate knotweed, chickweed, ripe grass and weed seed. The best insects to feed are ant pupae, white worms and small, cut-up mealworms. To properly nourish the young, the parent birds should become used to eating these supplements long before the breeding season starts. During the molt, the birds must have protein-rich foods, vitamins, minerals, soaked and just-sprouted small seeds. Avoid white millet, as it causes illness and even death among Gouldians.

Genus *Clytospiza (Brown Twin-spots)*

Brown Twin-spot *Clytospiza monteiri*

DESCRIPTION: Brown; head gray. Covert feathers of the upper tail red; tail black. Underside a reddish-brown, covered generously with white dots. Throat red (white on the female); the beak in both sexes is black, the eyes reddish-brown with a blue ring; legs brownish flesh-colored. Young just out of the nest don't have the spots on the throat and are more subdued in coloring; the "tear design" is not readily visible. Length: five inches (12 cm.).

DISTRIBUTION AND HABITAT: Central Africa. They tend to dwell in low bushes and on the ground, in grassland and savannas. In the wild, they prefer using the nests of other birds, with repairs and alterations. You might try to hang some used nests of other finches in your aviary to see if this would promote successful breeding.

CAPTIVITY: This species is suitable only for the more experienced fancier. As far as I know, no one has succeeded so far in breeding this bird in captivity, but I still believe this species is worthy of special attention. The best chance for future success is to furnish a roomy and especially quiet indoor aviary with sparse, live potted plants and a low level of humidity. On a number of occasions, a pair of birds had begun to build a nest and started to breed normally. Then, suddenly, without apparent cause, they abandoned the whole thing, frequently beginning a new home elsewhere. I would furnish several half-open nest boxes hung at differing heights on various walls of the aviary. For building material, furnish soft grass and hay, small leaves, down (for canary nests), leaf veins, and coconut fibers. For the rest, the care and feeding of these birds should be the same as for the genus *Hypargos*. The Brown Twin-spot *must* be acclimatized with special care after arrival in temperate

Chloebia gouldiae.

Diamond Finch

climate. Done properly, it shouldn't cause much difficulty. Be sure to keep them in a roomy facility at first, that is comfortably warm, without drafts and noise; inside aviaries are, obviously, the best. In winter, keep these birds indoors at a constant minimal temperature of 60° F (15° C). It is important at all times to keep the floor as clean as possible, as the birds like to peck in the sand for hours. Do tie some dry bushes and the like in the corners and at different heights along the wire mesh and wall; they love to hide there if they feel in danger or are too closely observed. After awhile, however, the birds become quite trusting and can be safely studied up close, except during the breeding season. They are fun to watch! They tend, as stated before, to stay on the ground a lot, where they move in little hops.

FOOD: See TWIN-SPOT genus *Hypargos.*

Genus *Cryptospiza* (Crimson- wings)

Red-faced Crimson-wing   *Cryptospiza reichenovii*

DESCRIPTION: Lore red; so are the areas around the eyes, the back, the wing coverts, the rump, the upper tail coverts and the flanks. Throat greenish; the rest of the body is grayish-green. Eyes dark brown with a red periophthalmic ring; beak black, legs brownish-black. The female has a yellowish eye ring. The colors of the entire coat of feathers are less intense. Young birds are brownish-green and the red on the back is still lacking. Length: five inches (12 cm.).

DISTRIBUTION AND HABITAT: The Cameroons (Africa) to the northern border of Angola; also in eastern Zaire, Uganda, Tanzania, and northern Mozambique. The species can be found higher than 6000 feet, in woodlands, particularly in the underbrush. There they hunt for small insects and various small seeds. They can be frequently found in thorn bushes, where they also will build their keg-shaped nests.

CAPTIVITY: All the Crimson-wings are mountain dwellers and therefore good candidates for outside aviaries because they can withstand the cold relatively well. However, when temperatures drop below 65° F (18° C), they ought to be brought indoors. All Crimson-wings become trusting toward their keeper in a very short time, and they are also friendly toward other small birds. The Red-faced Crimson-wing will breed in a well-planted aviary. The nest is built from grass, moss, and fibers. By preference, it is located in a dense shrub or occasionally in a half-open nest box.

FOOD: Provide a good mix of tropical seeds with a heavy proportion of small millet species. Panicum millet must be supplied daily, as well as grass and weed seed (also in sprouted form). Protein from animal sources is essential, especially in the breeding season.

113

Jackson's Crimson-wing *Cryptospiza jacksoni*

DESCRIPTION: Dark gray to black, especially on wings and tail; forehead and cheeks are red, as are back, rump and the covert feathers of the upper tail. Flanks somewhat orange red. Eyes dark brown, beak black, legs brown. The female can be distinguished from the male by a somewhat lesser intensity in the red of the head. Young birds lack this red and they possess an overall somewhat browner coat of feathers. Length: five inches (12 cm.).

DISTRIBUTION AND HABITAT: Central Africa. It lives in the mountains up to a height of 9,000 feet or more, principally in meadows and on the edges of forests.

CAPTIVITY: This species occasionally has been offered for sale, but I know of no cases where it has successfully been bred in captivity. Males have been observed doing a mating dance with a blade of grass in the bill, but mating and nest building did not ensue.

FOOD: Provide small millet and only in sprouted form. Then, offer weed and grass seed (in the ears) and a good supply of insects (ant pupae, white worms, fly larvae, and small, cut-up mealworms), plus a good brand of egg food for small tropical finches, which can be enriched with insects.

OTHER NAME: Dusky Crimson-wing.

Abyssinian Crimson-wing *Cryptospiza salvadorii*

DESCRIPTION: Like the Red-faced Crimson-wing, except there is no red on the head. In general, the feathers are a little browner. Length: five inches (12 cm.).

DISTRIBUTION AND HABITAT: East Africa, from Central Ethiopia to northern Tanzania. The birds are typical mountain dwellers, found up to a height of 9,000 feet.

CAPTIVITY: This species is best kept in an inside aviary with a rich planting (in pots). They are quite trusting and friendly toward birds of their own and other species. They will regularly breed in the aviary. The male does a mating dance, circling with a long blade of grass in the bill. For nesting material, furnish grass, fibers, and leaf veins. The keg-shaped nest generally is built in bushes, preferably thorny ones, but the birds will also move into half-open nest boxes.

FOOD: See RED-FACED CRIMSON-WING.

Shelley's Crimson-wing *Cryptospiza shelleyi*

DESCRIPTION: Upperpart red, with brownish-black on wings and upper-tail coverts. Tail black; underside yellowish-green. Eyes dark brown, as are the legs; the beak is red, a deviation from the other Crimson-wings. The female lacks the red in the head, which is yellowish-green instead. Length: five inches (14 cm.).

DISTRIBUTION AND HABITAT: The part of Central Africa east of Lake Victoria (Ruwenzori). The species lives 6,000 to 9,000 feet high in the mountain forests, in small, thorny bushes.

CAPTIVITY: This bird became available to the trade in the 1970s and has remained available at high prices. For more details see the above CRIMSON-WING species.

Genus *Emblema* (Fire-tailed Finches)

Painted Fire-tailed Finch *Emblema picta*

DESCRIPTION: Deep red on forehead, around eyes, chin, throat, breast, and rump. At the wing junction and the breast, the attractive deep red changes abruptly into black and dark brown. The belly has big, round spots that become smaller on the breast. Crown, neck, and wings are light greenish brown with primaries that are edged in darker green. Tail dark brown, banded in red. Eyes brown with a white eye ring; the lower mandible has a blue base, the upper bill is black with a red tip; legs flesh-colored. The female has considerably less red in the face and breast; the flanks are brownish. She lacks the white spots on breast and belly. Length: four inches (10 cm.).

DISTRIBUTION AND HABITAT: Australia, specifically the midwest and northwest; the Northern Territory; Central Australia; the northern part of South Australia and the northwestern parts of Queensland. The species occurs particularly in grassland, where it builds its nest, utilizing even little stones, pieces of bark and hard earth as building material.

CAPTIVITY: This is an extremely attractive bird, very suited to an aviary. It gets along well with other birds, including those of its own kind, and seldom gets into fights. The aviary should be well planted, a requirement of all Australian Grass Finches. Still, there should be open sandy spots as well. The birds tend to sleep on the ground or in low-hanging nest boxes.

The Painted Fire-tailed Finch builds nests in the plantings or in nest boxes, like Hartz canary nest boxes, provided they are placed low to the ground. It tends to use rough nesting material (as does the CRIMSON WAXBILL) such as leaves, rough dry grass, and bark, which are made into the foundation. The walls of the nest are made of small twigs, grass, leaf veins, and the like. For padding on the inside, it uses all types of small, soft feathers. Nest building can take all of two weeks. There is a small entryway leading to the inside of the nest, where the female lays four or five eggs; they hatch in 16 to 18 days, and the young leave the nest 20 to 25 days of age. After ten to twelve weeks, the young are adult, but should not be used for breeding until the following spring. Of course, they should be mated to unrelated birds to avoid inbreeding. The male has an interesting mating dance. With an averted head, he circles the female over and over.

The birds tend to be a little shy at first, but if cared for properly, they become quite trusting and are then readily encouraged to breed. For care and feeding, see the section on the STAR FINCH.

OTHER NAME: Mountain Finch.

Genus *Erythrura* (Parrot Finches)

Bamboo Munia   *Erythrura hyperythra*

DESCRIPTION: Upperside green; blue forehead. The upper tail-coverts are light green with a yellow reflection. Underside and cheeks brownish-yellow. Eyes red-brown, beak black-gray, legs pink. The female is visibly paler in tint and has a brown stripe across the bill; the male has a black stripe across the bill. The young are even paler in color than the female. Length: four inches (11 cm.).

DISTRIBUTION AND HABITAT: Malaya, Celebes, Java, Borneo (Indonesia), Luzon (Philippines), Lombok, Sumbawa, and Flores. It is a typical mountain dweller, reaching more than 9,000 feet above sea level. Birds live in pairs, even outside of the breeding season, or else they form small groups of two or three pairs. They eat principally all types of bamboo seed, grass and weed seeds.

CAPTIVITY: This beautiful bird was first imported into Germany in 1930 and then, in 1965, to Switzerland. There is no case of captive breeding on record.

FOOD: Includes all types of small millet, especially panicum millet. Also canary seed and grass and weed seeds. The birds utilize little of other seeds and they don't seem to want protein of animal origin. Some use egg and rearing food.

Tricolored Parrot Finch   *Erythrura tricolor*

DESCRIPTION: Green with a blue forehead, blue throat and cheeks, and a blue underside. Rump and upper tail-coverts and the tail itself are red. Eyes brownish-red, beak black, legs dark pink. The female is somewhat lighter in color. Fledglings lack the blue and have a pale green underside. Length: four inches (10 cm.).

DISTRIBUTION AND HABITAT: The islands of Timor and Tanimbar. Lives in mountain woods up to about 9,000 feet.

CAPTIVITY: This bird is unquestionably beautiful and resembles the BLUE-FACED PARROT FINCH. The species is imported from time to time but does not survive in captivity. No known cases of captive breeding have been recorded.

116

OTHER NAME: Blue-fronted Parrot Finch.

Red-eared Parrot Finch *Erythrura coloria*

DESCRIPTION: Green; blue forehead, face and cheeks. There is a unique half-moon shaped patch from the ear toward the neck. Rump, upper tail-coverts and the central tail feathers deep red. Eyes dark brown, beak black, legs gray flesh-colored. The female is duller and the young more so, with a green reflection on the upperside; they also lack the red and blue. After females reach a year of age, their colors brighten and then can no longer be distinguished, according to Prof. Ziswiler, from adult males; in any case, it pays to color-band young birds so that they can be sexed easily when they get older. Length: four inches (10 cm.).

DISTRIBUTION AND HABITAT: Mindanao (Philippines). Gonzales first discovered and caught this bird in 1960. It occurs in open places of light forests and along the rims of forests in the mountains. There it feeds on small insects and seeds.

CAPTIVITY: This bird was first imported into Europe in 1964, and a number of breeders then acquired some pairs which quickly were bred successfully. *E. coloria* is well-known in the USA. The species is not the least bit shy, and probably for this reason can easily be bred, provided breeding birds are properly acclimatized. They can be kept in roomy cages as well as aviaries. Provide half-open nest boxes, in which the birds will usually build a relatively large and rather rough nest from coconut fibers, grass, hay, and down. The clutch usually has two, occasionally three eggs, which are brooded for two weeks. Fledglings are still fed by their parents for 14 days after they leave the nest. After five months, the young acquire the adult colors. Care requirements are as for the RED-HEADED PARROT FINCH. Dr. Burkhard has identified this bird as one of the best breeders among the Parrot Finches; it is highly desirable to breed this bird with the greatest of care, because it is quite unlikely that many new imports will be possible.

FOOD: Furnish canary seed (also in sprouted form), panicum millet and small millet species. During the breeding season, add grass and weed seeds, even though not all birds will make much use of these. Also provide cut-up small mealworms, small ant pupae, white worms, boiled eggs (well diced), egg food and rearing food, and some greens, which the birds gladly consumer, especially in the breeding season.

Blue-faced Parrot Finch *Erythrura trichroa*

DESCRIPTION: Cheeks and forehead bright blue (which can differ somewhat among different varieties). Crown light green; the nape is darker. Upper tail-coverts are red. The wings are grass green. Primaries dark brown with light green and black edges. Tail feathers black with red borders. Many varieties don't have the attractive soft green, but there are all grades of intermediary colors up to nearly yellow, especially on the neck and on the thigh (tibia) feathers. Eyes dark brown, beak black, legs light gray-brown. The female is duller in coloration. Length: five inches (13 cm.).

DISTRIBUTION AND HABITAT: There are ten varieties of this species, occurring in Celebes, the Moluccas, New Guinea, northwestern Australia (the eastern part of Cape York), the Bismarck Archipelago (New Britain and New Ireland), Micronesia, the Salomon Islands, the New Hebrides, the Banks Islands, the Loyalty Islands, Baules Island and on Guadalcanal. The species live in the woods of the mountains up to 6,000 feet, and also in gardens and plantations, coastal plains, rain forests, and mangroves. They feed principally on grass and weed seeds. Their nest is preferably built high in the trees; it is rectangular in shape and constructed out of grass, moss, leaf veins, and dry leaves.

CAPTIVITY: This beautiful Parrot Finch is readily available in the trade. It requires about the same care as the Red-headed Parrot Finch. I personally believe that this bird is better raised in a roomy aviary than in cages. I know from experience that this bird is better able to withstand colder climates than many of the other Parrot Finches, once it has been properly acclimatized. The Blue-faced Parrot Finch is a good flyer even though it spends a good deal of time on the ground. It is an excellent breeder. It prefers a half-open nest box. The female lays three or four eggs that are brooded for 15 to 16 days. After six weeks, the young are completely independent and should preferably be removed from the parents. If the diet is adequate, the parents will then promptly start a new brood. As a matter of fact, this species is well-known to breed continuously if not stopped by removing nesting facilities. Only three broods per year should be allowed.

There are known crosses with the Pin-tailed Nonpareil and the Red-headed Parrot Finch. The young of such crosses are fertile, presenting an interesting opportunity for the breeder.

The birds do not tolerate temperatures under 65° F (18° C), so that it is important to move them to a heated facility for the winter months.

FOOD: As for the RED-HEADED PARROT FINCH.

Pink-billed Parrot Finch *Erythrura kleinschmidtii*

DESCRIPTION: Deep black on the forehead, the upper part of the feathers around the legs, the lores, chin, and ear coverts. The upperpart of the body is green. Rump and upper tail-coverts red; underside yellowish-green. Wings and tail are brownish-black. Eyes dark brown, beak pinkish-red, legs dark flesh-colored. The female is somewhat duller in coloration. Length: four inches (10 cm.).

Erythrura trichroa.

Erythrura coloria.

119

Erythrura prasina cock.

Erythrura cyaneovirens.

DISTRIBUTION AND HABITAT: Viti-Levu of the Fiji Islands. It is a mountain dweller par excellance and has been encountered up to 9,000 feet above sea level. It feeds on small seeds, fruits, insects, and flower buds.

CAPTIVITY: This is an extremely brightly colored bird that has been exported only rarely. I know of only some imports to Europe in the teens, and information on their care and feeding is lacking.

Royal Parrot Finch   *Erythrura cyaneovirens*

SUBSPECIES: Ornithologists distinguish four subspecies, but only two are in captive collections and then only in the hands of specialists. Dr. Burkhard acquired a Peale's Parrot Finch (*E. C. pealii*), which can be cared for and bred as the Red-headed Parrot Finch. It is an extremely good breeder that raised several sets of young in a season. It builds a free nest and also will use a half-open nest box. The clutches contain two to four eggs, which are brooded for about two weeks. While they breed, they should get much fruit and a rich assortment of insects. The bird originates in the plains of the Fiji Islands. It is green with a black head and a blue breast and throat. Forehead, crown, and the sides of the head are red. Only the high, trilling song of the male makes it possible to distinguish the sexes. Length: four inches (10 cm.).

Various subspecies of the Royal Parrot Finch—all with a short tail—are: *E. c. regia, E. c. efantensis,* and *E. c. serena.*

DESCRIPTION: The *E. c. regia* resembles the Peale's Parrot Finch, except that the blue areas are green; there also is more red, continuing far into the neck; the beak is reddish brown.

The *E. c. efantensis* and the *E. c. serena* also look amazingly similar to the Peale's Parrot Finch, but the mask (which is reminiscent of the Gouldian Finch) is marked with a broad, blue band. Length: four inches (11 cm.).

DISTRIBUTION AND HABITAT: Samoa, Fiji, and New Hebrides, in forest clearings, rice fields, grasslands, parks and gardens.

CAPTIVITY: The Royal Peale's Parrot Finch was first exported into Europe in 1934. It can be bred rather easily, provided the right nutrition is offered. Nests are built free in dense bushes. The clutch contains three eggs. Fledglings are fed by the male for three extra weeks after they leave the nest. Their youth molt starts at about two months of age and lasts two to three months!

FOOD: This species utilizes a lot of fruit every day and also should get canary seed, grass and weed seeds, and various small millets. It is not easy to convert these birds to a seed diet. They require sprouted seeds throughout the year. In their country of origin they live principally on the seeds of date trees.

OTHER NAME: Royal Peale's Parrot Finch.

Pintailed Nonpareil   *Erythrura prasina*

DESCRIPTION: Forehead, the area around the eye, cheeks, throat and part of the breast ink-blue. Around the beak, the color darkens to black. Nape, neck, back and wings dark grass green. Primaries black, edged in yellow. Uppertail coverts and tail scarlet. Underside yellow with a red sheen, so that one seems to see a dim orange. Belly almost orange-red. Eyes dark brown, beak black, legs pink. The female has no red on the breast and further is less brightly colored. Length: six inches (15 cm.).

DISTRIBUTION AND HABITAT: Java, Borneo, Sumatra (Indonesia), Malaysia, Laos and Thailand. The birds live in groups ranging from a few pairs to rather large flocks in the underbrush at the forest edge. There have been many reports of birds in the rice fields, where they can be a true pest. They "crawl" around in rough branches and the like, so that their nails wear down regularly. So in the aviary, be sure to provide them with reeds and flagstones to help them keep their nails trimmed.

CAPTIVITY: This beautiful bird is really well suited only to experienced fanciers; it is difficult to keep alive and in good condition. Acclimatizing it requires much effort and experience. Frequently birds shipped from their native land are fed principally on paddy rice during the journey, and new arrivals suffer from one-sided feeding. They require much vitamin B and D. Immediately after arrival, they must be housed in roomy flight cages, kept at a constant minimal temperature of 77° F (25° C). The cages must be equipped with infrared lamps. Once the birds recover after a few weeks of special care, the temperature can be dropped to 68° F (20° C). You will be able to tell that the birds feel "happy" when you see them make agile movements and you hear the male singing. If it is possible to acclimatize the birds in inside aviaries, I would prefer this above large flight cages. Even if the care is first-rate, don't expect the birds to become trusting even though they are curious and will allow you to approach them closely.

Breeding is a real task, especially considering that the birds molt twice a year. The molt, however, goes fast, lasting about two to three weeks. The mating dance is well worth studying. The male repeatedly makes races toward the female, meanwhile making small bows with his whole body and beating his tail from left to right. Sometimes he runs sideways like a crab for several paces. He performs his song with enthusiasm and sometimes it looks as if he whispers something into his mate's ear. The couple builds a sizable nest from fibers, grass, leaves, leaf veins, and the like. They rarely use nest boxes. The female lays two to five eggs, which she broods for about two weeks. After three weeks, the young leave the nest. The temperature must be maintained around 77° F (25° C), and infrared lamps should be used during the entire brooding period. I have found that it is best to keep three to five pairs in a single roomy aviary to achieve successful breeding.

122

FOOD: Provide paddy rice and an abundance of oats, canary seed, silver millet and panicum millet, plus wheat (which is very important). All these seeds may also be furnished as sprouts. Put a multivitamin in the drinking water. Also furnish a daily supply of cuttle bone, grit and limestone, charcoal, grass and weed seed, greens like chickweed and lettuce, apple, cherry, orange, and pieces of cucumber. After some time, you can get away from paddy rice altogether. Especially during the breeding season, don't forget to supply animal protein, such as cut-up mealworms, white worms, ant pupae, commercial egg and rearing food.

Red-headed Parrot Finch   *Erythrura psittacea*

DESCRIPTION: Red face, upperparts of breast, rump, and tail; rest parrot-green. Eyes dark brown, beak black, legs light gray-brown. The female is duller with less red on the face. Length: five inches (12 cm.).

DISTRIBUTION AND HABITAT: New Caledonia, in grassland and scrubbery.

CAPTIVITY: This is a truly bright-colored bird, which is exceptionally suited for a roomy aviary with a lot of plants. It must not be exposed to temperatures below 65° F (18° C), so that in the winter months it must always be moved to a heated facility. The best breeding results are achieved in a large indoor aviary, equipped with nest boxes of at least seven inches (18 cm.) on each side. The birds build a rather sizeable nest from grass, fibers, leaf veins, and the like. They lay clutches of three to five eggs, of which there usually are a few infertile ones. Incubation time, 13 days. After 21 days, the young fly out, and they sleep in brotherly (and sisterly) love close together in the low plantings. There is no objection to keeping grown-up young with the parents. This species doesn't take nest inspections very well. When bred in small cages, it is of the utmost importance to take the young away from the father two weeks after they have left the nest; he can become hostile towards them.

FOOD: Includes various millets, canary seed, niger seed, poppyseed, ripe and unripe grass and weed seed, and oats. Also furnish a rich variety of greens, such as lettuce and chickweed; fruit, such as figs, dates, and oranges; and— this is important—a lot of animal protein, such as ant pupae, larvae, white worms, small, cut-up mealworms, wax moths, tubifex, water fleas, and other water insects, plus a good brand egg- and rearing-food. Some birds also will reluctantly accept old white bread soaked in milk or water.

Genus *Estrilda* (Waxbills or Typical Waxbills)

Lavender Waxbill   *Estrilda caerulescens*

DESCRIPTION: Gray-blue, darker on the back, lighter on the cheeks and throat. Underside black with white alone the flanks. Rump, undertail coverts, and tail red. Little black periophthalmic ring; black lores. Eyes brown, beak red with a black tip, legs light brown. The female is generally less intense, which allows sexing without much difficulty. Length: four inches (10 cm.).

DISTRIBUTION AND HABITAT: From Senegal to the Cameroons in West Africa. It is found particularly in grassland and steppes, picking around in low bushes and clumps of grass in search of insects and grass and weed seed. It also is encountered frequently in gardens, parks, and even along busy highways.

CAPTIVITY: This species is a rather tender bird that always requires special attention from its keeper. The birds don't look very robust when they arrive from overseas, and they require special attention also at that time. But in somewhat heated vitrines and indoor aviaries they can develop quite nicely.

Lavender waxbills are amont the best acrobats in the bird world. They are uniformly cheerful and lively and always ready to perform their simple song. The mating call of the male distinguishes the sexes, which otherwise are somewhat hard to tell apart, especially when young. Lavender Waxbills perform a pleasant night-time routine. Once the sun has set, the male and female sit close together at their usual roosting place, nod good night with definite head movements, and utter a somewhat monotonous but pleasant-sounding "chew-chew-chew." The summoning calls differ between the sexes; the male calls with a "shee-tooey," while the female utters "shee-shee." If you separate the two, these summoning calls can be heard constantly.

In the wild, as well as in the aviary, Lavender Waxbills build a round nest with a small, narrow entryway near the bottom. It is desirable to provide adequate space for this species. Putting them in cages that are too small often results in their losing head and neck feathers from plucking. The same problem also occurs in recently imported individuals.

Lavender waxbills are among the best acrobats in the bird world. They have occurred in indoor aviaries and in garden aviaries with favorable weather (Florida, Southern California). They do well in groups. Be sure to furnish them separate sleeping nests and baskets; put some nesting material inside, so that they have some cover against the cold at night.

As an aside on the subject of breeding—there has been repeated success in crossing the Lavender Waxbill with the Red-billed Fire Finch.

The female lays three to five eggs (see RED-EARED WAXBILL). At about two weeks of age, the young leave the nest, but are still fed by the parents for a considerable period of time. For some time, the young have gray-blue papillae (mouth markings). Once the young are independent (at about a month of age), remove them from the parents. They unfortunately tend to do some feather picking, especially if the facility is too cramped—as I said earlier. To minimize the problem, add extra cuttle bone, finely ground egg shell, and vitamins A and D.

FOOD: A good commercial seed mix for small finches, as well as universal food, a good variety of egg mixture, ant pupae, egg yolk, finely cut

Estrilda caerulescens.

Erythrura psittacea, juvenile.

Erythrura psittacea, adults.

mealworms, white worms, greens (lettuce, endive, chicory, chickweed, etc.), and millet spray. The ant pupae can be given fresh as well as in the dry form. This food is indispensable, particularly during the breeding season.

OTHER NAMES: Red-tailed Lavender, Lavender Finch.

Cinderella Waxbill *Estrilda thomensis*

DESCRIPTION: Light grayish-blue with a red reflection on breast and back. The black lore continues past the eyes into the neck. Rump and upper tail-coverts red, as are the flanks. Halfway across the stomach, the color changes to black, which continues across the abdomen. Eyes brown, beak red with a black tip and black edges, legs black. The female has less red, especially along the flanks. On the breast, she may lack the red coloration altogether. The abdomen and the lower covert feathers of the tail are more black-gray. The song is almost identical to that of the Lavender Waxbill. Length: four inches (10 cm.).

DISTRIBUTION AND HABITAT: Western Angola to the Cunene River. Occurs in mountainous, wooded areas up to 3,000 feet high, especially along the edge of forests and in clearings. The species lives on half-ripe grass and weed seed and many types of small insects and spiders.

CAPTIVITY: Until 1963, when several individuals were sighted, it was thought that this species was extinct. They were imported into Europe and bred successfully in 1970. They must be kept in a roomy inside aviary with the temperature around 85° F (30° C). Further care and feeding are identical to recommendations for the LAVENDER WAXBILL (immediately preceding).

OTHER NAME: São Thomé Waxbill.

Dufresne's Waxbill *Estrilda melanotis*

SUBSPECIES: Ornithologists distinguish several subspecies. Best-known among these is the Abyssinian Green Waxbill (*E. m. quartinia*), which has been offered in the trade since 1960 (a little earlier in Europe). The species is not imported very often, but it can be raised successfully, particularly in vitrines. Acclimatization, however, takes a lot of care; use infrared lamps to keep the temperature to 77° F (25° C) for two months, after which you can reduce it to 68° F (20° C). Abyssinians breed well and make good use of half-open nest boxes. They like fine nesting material, like dry grass and sisal. The nest bowl is furnished with small, soft feathers. Eggs are brooded 13 days. The young are raised almost entirely on insects or substitute animal proteins. After at least 20 days, the young fly out, but they return to the parental nest for several nights. After 15 to 20 days they are adult and can be safely separated from the parents.

126

The color is green, the underparts are yellow, the rump red, as are the upper tail coverts. The upper beak is black, the lower red. The female is a little less intense in coloration.

Another subspecies is the Green Waxbill (*E. m. kilimensis*), which also is imported only rarely. Don't confuse this bird with the Green Avadavat. The Green Waxbill is gray with a greenish-gray back. Rump and upper tail coverts are red. Throat clear white; lower body yellowish-white. Flanks yellow-green, wings brown, tail black. The beak resembles that of the Abyssinian. The female is a bit lighter in hue on the underside.

DESCRIPTION (nominate form): Head, breast and flanks gray; wings and tail brown-gray. The rest of the underside beige-to-yellow. Throat and cheeks black. Eyes brown, upper mandible black, lower bill red, legs black. In the female the black mask is lacking. Length: four inches (10 cm.).

DISTRIBUTION AND HABITAT: Ethiopia and the southeastern Sudan. Among the subspecies, the Abyssinian, of course, comes from Abyssinia. The Green Waxbill comes from northeastern Africa; two other subspecies, *E. m. melanotis* and *E. m. bocagei*, are from East and South Africa, from Ethiopia to Angola and the Cape. All species occur in mountain forests, preferably in low bushes. They also are encountered in gardens and parks, particularly in hedges. They nest in bushes and hedges, constructing mainly with grass. They feed on all types of seeds and small insects and spiders.

CAPTIVITY: This little bird is hard to obtain, although the better dealers do have a few each year. It is known for its fast movements but it certainly is not aggressive, even though some people may not agree. I believe that it can properly be housed with other small birds.

Treat this bird right and it quickly becomes quite trusting. It is an excellent cage and aviary bird. In an outdoor aviary, it does better than most as it is quite hardy. Still, I definitely recommend moving it out of the garden aviary into a lightly heated facility during the winter.

The general care is similar to what is recommended for the two previous species. Let me add, however, that Dufresne's Waxbills are sensitive to disturbances during the breeding season, so leave them in peace. They are easy to start breeding if there are enough live plantings and bushes in the aviary. They prefer to build a free nest, although they do use nest boxes and baskets. Incubation time: 12-14 days. The three or four young leave the nest after 21 days. At that time they still have black bills; after three months they come into their adult plumage.

FOOD: Provide all types of small millet species. Further, furnish grass and weed seed, half-ripe and soaked. A rich variation of greens is highly important. In the breeding season especially, and also at other times, they should have a daily ration of all types of animal protein. Offer food on a little

127

platform, say about 20 inches (50 cm.) high, because the birds don't like to be on the ground.

OTHER NAME: Yellow-bellied Waxbill.

Black-cheeked Waxbill   *Estrilda erythronotos.* See also *E. charmosyna,* p. 105.

DESCRIPTION: Breast, flanks and abdomen red, slowly grading into black. Crown dark gray; cheeks, neck, and throat light gray. Around the eyes a black band that also runs under the lower beak. It seems as if the bird has a moustache, and the French call it "l'astrilde à moustaches noires" (waxbill with a black moustache). Primaries doe-brown to gray-brown. The rest of the wing gray to white, with brown cross bars. Back and rump bright red. Tail black. Eyes red, beak a brilliant steel-blue to black at the tip, legs black. The color of the female is a little less intense; the underside is more grayish-black. There is no red on the back and breast; other red areas are less bright. The birds have a rather monotonous song that goes "doo-duh-doo-oo-oo." Length: five inches (12 cm.).

DISTRIBUTION AND HABITAT: Southern, southwestern, and eastern Africa, from Kenya and Uganda to Tanzania. It is a typical steppe-dweller that builds a pretty, keg-shaped nest out of straw, grass, and wool. The nest, which has a long entryway, is build in thorny bushes.

CAPTIVITY: This species is one of the foster parents of the Pintail Whydah (*Vidua macroura*) and the Senegal Combassou (*Hypochera* [Vidua] *hypocherina*). It is difficult to obtain a good breeding pair. First, they may not be available at all because there is no regular supply chain. Secondly, they are expensive. And beyond that, it is hard to sex them so that you always must be sure to have an arrangement with the seller to allow an exchange if you didn't acquire a true pair. You can tell the male by his mating dance and his piercing cry, "toooeyt-toooeyt."

I have raised them successfully in a regular community aviary. The birds build a keg-shaped nest. The two clutches I raised had five white eggs that were brooded 13 days, in turn by the male and female.

The birds love to sit in the sun, where they will stay for hours, holding their wings low. If you want to raise these birds indoors, you must definitely work with infrared lamps. They like to go to searching about in dense bushes and also spend a lot of time on the ground. The Black-cheeked Waxbill is particularly sensitive to dampness. That is why it's important to raise the surface of the garden aviary above that of the surrounding yard, so that the surface doesn't stay wet after a rain shower. Further, the sleeping coop has to be absolutely watertight, and damp-free, too.

I consider this tender species suited only for experienced breeders, as the birds are hard to keep in good condition, not to speak of breeding. Success in breeding is dependent on a good source of insects for food. Before the start of

The familiar Red-cheeked Cordon Bleu *(Uraeginthus bengalus)* is widely admired in aviculture around the world. This species is sexually dimorphic with only the male having red ear patches.

Photo by author

Gray-headed Silverbill *(Odontospiza* [or *Lonchura*] *caniceps).*   *Photo by author*

Black-cheeked Waxbill *(Estrila erythronotos).*   *Photo by au*

Green-backed Twin-spot *(Mandingoa nitidula).* *Photo by author*

ola Cordon Bleu *(Uraeginthus angolensis).* *Photo by author*

African Silverbills *(Euodice* [or *Lonchura*] *malabarica cantans).* Photo by author

Black-headed Munia (Lonchura malacca atricapilla). Photo by author

Blue-faced Parrot Finch (Erythrura trichroa).
Photo by author

Masked Finch *(Poephila personata).*   *Photo by author*

St. Helena Waxbill *(Estrilda astrild).*   *Photo by author*

Blue-headed Waxbill *(Uraeginthus cyanocephalus).*
Photo by author

Long-tailed Finch *(Poephila acuticauda).*   *Photo by author*

Diamond Sparrows *(Emblema [Zonaeginthus] guttata)*. *Photo by autho*

the breeding season, supply spiders, ant pupae, small mealworms, white worms, universal food and the like.

In the winter months, house them in a lightly heated facility, preferably with an infrared lamp. Even in summer, I think it best to keep the birds at a temperature about 77° F (25° C), if they have arrived recently. You can gradually drop the temperature to 68° F (20° C).

On nice, sunny days, they can make good use of an outside aviary, but they need to have a sleeping coop year round. They are quite trusting, so that they can be kept indoors in roomy cages; there, however, you can't count on successful breeding, which is chancy anywhere. They build free nests and also make use of nest boxes and baskets. The problem with them is that after several days of steady brooding, they may abandon their eggs; or, they may stop feeding their young after they are half raised! In any case, a peaceful surrounding is of the first importance, as is proper diet. It is also wise to change the drinking water daily and add several drops of disinfectant to it.

The mating dance is interesting to watch. The male dances around the female in full song, with a blade of grass in the beak. If the blade is long, he holds it off the ground (or off the branch) with one of his legs.

FOOD: All types of small millets, grass and weed seed, and a rich variety of animal protein. They also accept flower leaves. The general feeding is like that for the RED-EARED WAXBILL.

Fawn-breasted Waxbill *Estrilda paludicola*

DESCRIPTION: Upperparts brown, darker on back and wings, often with a somewhat red reflection. Underparts red-brown, cheeks gray, belly white. Tail black with white edges; upper tail coverts red. Eyes brown, beak red, legs brown. The female doesn't have as intense a red coloration. The young are generally grayer and still have a black bill. The song is a loud chirp; they also use a variety of communication calls that are performed by chirping and whistling. Length: four inches (11 cm.).

DISTRIBUTION AND HABITAT: From Ethiopia to deep in the southern Sudan, further to Zambia and from there westward up to Angola. Also along the Congo up to the Niger delta. They live along water, in swamps and the like, where they feel at home in the grass and reeds. The nest is built on or close to the ground and resembles that of the Red-eared Waxbill. In the breeding season they occur in pairs or small groups; afterwards, they form large flocks at times.

CAPTIVITY: This bird looks deceptively like the Orange-cheeked Waxbill, only it is a bit larger. After proper acclimatization, it proves to be a strong bird that will build a free nest in dense bushes without much difficulty. It also will breed in nest boxes and baskets and even tolerates your checking on the nest, provided you don't do it too often.

You can achieve good results housing several pairs (at least three) together in one facility. They live on the ground and like to crawl in grass and reeds. For further details on breeding, consult the section on the ORANGE-CHEEKED WAXBILL and the RED-EARED WAXBILL.

FOOD: Consult the section on the RED-EARED WAXBILL.

Orange-cheeked Waxbill *Estrilda melpoda*

DESCRIPTION: Mouse-brown, lighter on crown and nape. Underparts grayish-white. Rump orange-red, tail blackish-blue, cheeks light orange, lores orange-red. Eyes brown, beak red, legs pinkish. The cheek spots of the female are often somewhat smaller; she is, in general, also duller in coloration. Only the male sings. The young have black beaks and possess more brown and black in their plumage. Length: four inches (10 cm.).

DISTRIBUTION AND HABITAT: Western central Africa, in three subspecies. Some years ago, escaped aviary birds established themselves in the Caribbean. This species lives in light forests, grassland, agricultural areas, large parks, and gardens. During the breeding season in pairs, outside this time in small groups.

CAPTIVITY: A true pair fairly often comes to breed in a well-planted garden aviary, with low bushes and high grass. The birds like to construct their oval-shaped nests about five feet (two meters) from the ground; they also prefer the half-open nest boxes in which they build a round nest of grass, wool, horse hair, plant fibers, etc. Two males or two females may act as a pair. The female lays two to four, sometimes up to seven, eggs; incubation time, 11-12 days. After two or three weeks the young leave the nest. Don't disturb the breeding birds, as they are very sensitive to disturbances. The young assume their full plumage after the first moult, which is after approximately seven weeks. Acclimatization takes some time; house the birds in large cages or indoor aviaries (minimum temperature 73° F or 23° C). Cross-breedings with Red-eared Waxbills and Common Waxbills are possible.

FOOD: As RED-EARED WAXBILL. In order to achieve breeding successes a variety of small insects is absolutely essential.

Common Waxbill *Estrilda astrild*

SUBSPECIES: There are various subspecies (18) of which the most important are:

E. a. sactae helenae, with red on tail and wings (St. Helena); *E. a. angolensis,* with much red on tail, wings and belly (from Cameroun to Loango); *E. a. damarensis,* with light brown upperparts; this subspecies is paler than the nominate form and *E. a. ngamiensis* (from Niger to Zambezi); *E. a. minor,* with white ear patches (Nubia to Zambezi); *E. a. occidentalis,* with red on

138

back and belly; the brown colors are lighter than on *E. astrild* (from Cameroun to Loango); *E. a. ngamiensis,* an extremely pale colored subspecies (Ngamiland); *E. a. cavendishi,* with a pale throat, and pale ear patches; this subspecies is smaller than *damarensis* (Mozambique, and eastern Rhodesia northwards to Kenya).

DESCRIPTION: The nominate form (*E. astrild*) has a dark gray-brown crown and nape; the back is somewhat lighter. Cheeks, throat and partly the breast light brownish-white; red stripe through the eyes. Red belly (not as intense in females); flanks and underparts dark gray-brown, washed in pink. Practically the whole body is covered with fine dark brown bars, except for throat and ear patches. Eyes brown, beak red, legs brownish-red. The female is somewhat smaller, with lighter markings and with less pink on the abdomen. Length: five inches (12 cm.).

DISTRIBUTION AND HABITAT: Africa, south of the Sahara, the Malagasy Republic (Madagascar), Mauritius; and St. Helena and New Caledonia; this species is now feral in Portugal and parts of Spain (Europe!). They live primarily in grassland and cultivated areas. The Common Waxbills were imported in the 19th century in St. Helena.

CAPTIVITY: In the aviary the male builds a bullet-shaped nest from moss, grass, hay, small fibers, hair and feathers in a thick bush or in half-open nest boxes. Nest boxes should be hung high. The female lays one to four eggs; incubation time 10-13 days. After two weeks the young leave the nest but will be nourished by the parents for yet another ten to fourteen days. It is advisable to house only one pair in a community aviary to avoid troubles, as they can be rather aggressive during that time, even towards larger birds. All *Estrildae*-species must have access to a daily water bath.

FOOD: See RED-EARED WAXBILL. Animal protein is essential throughout the year, but especially in the breeding season.

OTHER NAME: St. Helena Waxbill.

Crimson-rumped Waxbill *Estrilda rhodopyga*

DESCRIPTION: Crown blue-gray; cheeks and throat somewhat lighter. Tail red; undertail coverts dark brown with a reddish sheen. Red eye stripe. Underparts white-yellow; wings and back dark brown-gray. Central tail feathers with crimson edges as well as the inner secondaries. Very similar to *E. troglodytes.* Eyes brown, beak and legs dark brown. The red eye stripe in the female is smaller and the light blue-gray throat patches are less extensive. Young birds are browner and don't have much red in their plumage. Length: five inches (12 cm.).

DISTRIBUTION AND HABITAT: East Africa; in grassland, farmland, open country, and near villages; in small groups. There are two subspecies.

Estrilda rhodopyga.

Estrilda astrild.

CAPTIVITY: These birds must be acclimatized with care (minimum temperature approximately 86° F; 30° C), but after that period they are excellent for a garden aviary, although females are known to suffer easily from egg-binding. In an aviary as well as in the wild they often take the nests of the Orange-cheek Waxbill (*E. melpoda*) but also build their own nests from wool, plant fibers, small feathers, grass, hay and the like. They also construct—like *E. melpoda* and *E. troglodytes*—small nests in the immediate vicinity of the breeding nest; these can be regarded as decoys. For more breeding details see *E. troglodytes*.

FOOD: As *E. troglodytes*; egg food is essential although not always appreciated. Various small insects and spiders are a must throughout the year but especially during the breeding season, as are grass and weed seed (fresh and sprouted).

OTHER NAMES: Rosy-rumped Waxbill, Ruddy Waxbill and Sundervall's Waxbill.

Black-cheeked Waxbill   *Estrilda charmosyna*. See also *E. erythronotos*, p. 101.

DESCRIPTION: Similar to another species of the same name, *E. erythronotos*. The throat is grayish-red, as are breast, belly and undertail coverts. Length: five inches (12 cm.).

DISTRIBUTION AND HABITAT: From Cameroon to Kenya and Tanzania; Somalia and east to Tanzania; in scrub country.

CAPTIVITY: Care and management essentials are similar to those required by *E. erythronotos*.

OTHER NAME: Pink-bellied Waxbill.

Black-headed Waxbill   *Estrilda atricapilla*

DESCRIPTION: Crown glossy black, as are the tail feathers. Back dark brown with black feather tips. Rump red, wings dark brown with black specks. Underparts blue-gray, darker toward the undertail coverts. Eyes dark brown, beak dark gray with a yellow spot on the lower mandible, legs dark brown. Young birds are fully colored after approximately six weeks. Length: five inches (10 cm.).

DISTRIBUTION AND HABITAT: From Cameroun to Kenya and Tanzania; along and in forests, and close to roads and water.

CAPTIVITY: This species looks very similar to the Black-crowned Waxbill. It is, however, rarely imported. It is an excellent and lively bird for large cages or well-planted aviaries, where it is friendly toward most other small African finches. In the breeding season it sometimes is somewhat quarrelsome. During fall and winter this species is best housed in an indoor facility with an average room temperature.

FOOD: During the breeding season a rich animal protein diet is absolutely necessary; also small millets, spray millet, grass and weed seeds throughout the year.

Gray Waxbill *Estrilda perreini*

DESCRIPTION: Almost similar to the Lavender Waxbill, but darker. Tail, undertail coverts and chin black. Rump and uppertail coverts red; white dots on the flanks. Eyes dark brown, beak red with a black tip, legs light brown. The female is duller and more grayish, especially on the undertail coverts. Length: five inches (11 cm.).

DISTRIBUTION AND HABITAT: From Zaire to southwestern Tanzania and eastern South Africa. Found in and near woodland and forests, in trees and bushes in which they build round nests.

CAPTIVITY: This bird is fairly well-known in aviculture. It must be acclimatized with the greatest of care (minimal 77° F; 25° C); humidity 60-70%). The species is friendly toward other small finches. In order to achieve breeding results, house three or more pairs together in a well-planted aviary. For more details see BLACK-RUMPED WAXBILL (*E. troglodytes*).

FOOD: All small millets, millet spray, grass and weed seeds (fresh and germinated), a variety of greens, cuttle bone, and animal protein, especially in the breeding season.

OTHER NAME: Black-tailed Lavender Finch.

Red-eared Waxbill *Estrilda troglodytes*

DESCRIPTION: Neck and back dark gray-brown; cheeks beige-brown; crimson eye-line; wings dark gray-brown with black-edged primaries. Tail black. Throat whitish with a vague pink sheen. Underparts grayish-white with a pink sheen, and reddish on the belly. The red color becomes more intense during the breeding season. Eyes light brown, beak red, legs brown-gray. The red in females is less intense. Length: four inches (10 cm.).

DISTRIBUTION AND HABITAT: From Senegal to Sudan and northern Ethiopia. A subspecies, which has more red in the underparts, lives in the southwestern parts of Africa: the Arabian Waxbill (*E. t. rufibarba*). The Red-eared Waxbill is found in semi-arid areas and swamps.

CAPTIVITY: An excellent, lively cage and aviary bird which is especially at home in large facilities. They are friendly towards other finches. The female lays three to five eggs in a nest box or in a free-standing, bullet-shaped nest in a bush. It is constructed from grass, wool, moss, fibers, and small feathers. The eggs hatch after 11-12 days; incubation is alternately performed by male and female, generally, for periods of three hours each. After two weeks the young leave the nest but accept food from their parents for another ten days. Young birds still have black beaks, and all red coloration is missing. After six weeks the youngsters are fully colored. During the breeding period the color of the male becomes more intense red, and his eyebrows become darker. He then goes through his display, holding a blade of grass or something similar in his beak, dancing in circles around the female. As soon as the breeding season starts it is advisable to separate the various pairs and give them each their own large aviary, which must be well-planted. The partners communicate with a harsh "pee-chee, pee-chee." During fall and winter the birds must be housed indoors at a minimum temperature of 77° F (25° C). Cross-breedings are possible with various finches; the most common ones are with the Orange-cheeked Waxbill, Red-cheeked Cordon Bleu, African Golden-breasted Waxbill, and Crimson-rumped Waxbill.

FOOD: Various small millets, spray millet, grass and weed seed (fresh and sprouted), canary grass seed, niger seed, greens (lettuce, spinach, dandelion, chickweed, etc.), ant pupae, white worms, maggots, daphnias, cut-up mealworms, fruit flies, green flies, egg and rearing food, cuttle bone and vitamins.

OTHER NAMES: Black-rumped Waxbill, Gray Waxbill, and Pink-cheeked Waxbill.

Black-crowned Waxbill *Estrilda nonnula*

DESCRIPTION: Almost similar to Black-headed Waxbill, but with less or no red on the flanks, especially after the birds have been living in captivity for some time. The black beak has red edges. Young birds are primarily brown. The bird's song consists of a series of high chirping calls. Length: four inches (10 cm.).

DISTRIBUTION AND HABITAT: From Cameroon to southern Sudan and Kenya; along the edges of forests, in savannas and farmland; also fairly high in the mountains. They search for seeds and insects in bushes and on the ground, during the breeding season in pairs, but outside this period in small groups.

CAPTIVITY: A charming, lively bird that is exceptionally well-suited for cage and aviary life. During the day they like to take sun-baths. For more details see preceding species.

FOOD: As the RED-EARED WAXBILL. They have a special fancy for poppy seed (supply only very small quantities!), and the seeds of dandelion as well as various small insects and spiders. A large selection of insects is especially necessary during the breeding season and molting time. Grit, calcium, and vitamins are musts for this species.

Genus *Euodice* (Silverbills)

143

Indian Silverbill Munia *Euodice [Lonchura] malabarica*

DESCRIPTION: Light brown; rump white; breast and throat yellowish-brown; underparts white. Wings light brown (like back), with darker primaries. Uppertail coverts white with black edges. Eyes dark brown, beak silver gray-blue (darker in *E. cantans*); the lower mandible somewhat darker, legs gray-blue, often with a pinkish sheen. The sexes are alike. Length: five inches (11 cm.).

DISTRIBUTION AND HABITAT: India, Sri Lanka and Afghanistan, mainly in open country, gardens, parks, orchards, savannas, but usually close to water. The birds breed in low, dense bushes; often two clutches in one nest. One pair usually has a large clutch of six to eight eggs, sometimes ten.

CAPTIVITY: An excellent cage and aviary bird; it doesn't demand much and is a prolific breeder. The bird looks very similar to the African Silverbill. Sexes can only be distinguished by the almost inaudible, somewhat muttering song of the male, and during the mating season when he dances around his bride with a grass stem in his beak. A true pair will build a free, small nest in a bush or in a nest box, but also like to use old weavers' nests, which they provide with a long and narrow entrance. They are inoffensive towards their own kind as well as towards other small finches. Therefore they are very suitable in a community aviary. The female may lay up to 12 eggs; both parents incubate the eggs which hatch after 12-13 days. After 21 days the young leave the nest. Don't allow more than three broods per season.

FOOD: See AFRICAN SILVERBILL.

OTHER NAMES: Silverbill, and White-throated Munia.

African Silverbill *Euodice [Lonchura] malabarica cantans*

DESCRIPTION: Light sandy brown with indistinct little stripes. Darker on tail and wings; light on belly and undertail coverts. The sexes are alike. Young are duller and browner; their beak is brownish. Eyes dark brown, upper mandible gray-blue (not as dark as in *E. malabarica*), lower mandible light gray-blue, legs blue-gray or pinkish. Length: five inches (11 cm.).

DISTRIBUTION AND HABITAT: West and central Africa, in four subspecies. Their habitats are savannas, farmland, and near human settlement in gardens, parks, and orchards. The nests are built under roofs and/or in the walls of the huts occupied by the natives; also in low, thick shrubs or in old weavers' nests.

CAPTIVITY: This species, excellent for large cages and community aviaries, is easy to keep and a steady breeder. The best breeding successes are obtained in well-planted outdoor aviaries, although these facilities must be located in a quiet place, as breeding pairs are very susceptible to disturbances. Avoid, therefore, nest inspection. The female lays (only!) three or four eggs; both

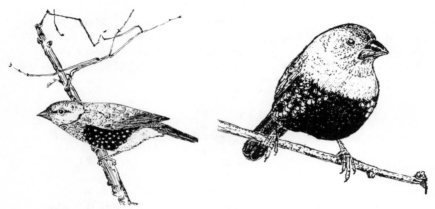

Euschistospiza dybowskii.

Hypargos niveo guttatus cock.

Euodice m. malabarica.

145

sexes incubate them for 12-13 days. After 21 days the young leave the nest. For further details see preceding species. Crossings are possible with Bengalese, Indian Silverbill, Common Waxbill, and Rufous-backed Mannikin. When care and management are up to par this species becomes very friendly toward its keeper; during the winter months they must be housed inside at room temperature (minimal 65° F; 18° C).

FOOD: During the year but especially during the breeding season various grass and weed seeds (fresh and sprouted), small millets, and a commercial seed mix for small finches are essential. Furthermore, greens, egg and rearing food, animal protein, white bread soaked in water or milk, cuttle bone, vitamins and minerals.

Genus *Euschistospiza* (Dusky Twin-spots)

Dybowski's Twin-spot *Euschistospiza dybowskii*

DESCRIPTION: Head, neck and partly the breast green-grayish; back red. Wings dark gray-black; flanks black with white drop-design; underparts dark brown; tail black. Eyes dark brown, periophthalmic ring red, beak black, legs gray-brown. Females are duller in coloration and have more gray-brown on the underparts; the drop-design is more grayish. Young birds are generally grayer, and the red on back and rump is indistinct; the drop-design is also missing. Both sexes have a pleasant song, consisting of tinkling, whistling and chirping tones; the female only sings more softly than the male and her concerts won't last as long. Length: five inches (12 cm.).

DISTRIBUTION AND HABITAT: Central Africa. An inhabitant of rain forests, where it lives close to water. It looks for food in low bushes and on the ground. I have seen this bird in pastures, and along not-too-busy roads as well.

CAPTIVITY: This species is very well suited for large, well-planted indoor vitrines and aviaries. It must be acclimatized with care. The bird may be housed outdoors during warm summer weather, but belongs indoors in the fall and winter months (minimum temperatures 50° F; 10° C). The bottom of the vitrine or aviary must be covered with grass sods. Due to its nervous nature, this bird is not suitable for cages. It usually comes to brood if there is enough choice in nest boxes and bunches of heather. The mating dance is almost similar to the African Silverbill's; the male often waves to his future bride with a small feather or a blade of grass. The female lays three or four eggs; both sexes incubate the eggs, which hatch after 12-13 days. The young leave the nest when approximately 23 days old. After the young have left the nest they will be nourished for another two weeks by, primarily, the male. After about four months the young are fully colored.

FOOD: See MELBA FINCH. It is important to remember that birds of this genus only take food from the bottom of their vitrine or aviary, and not from feeders hung against the wall. They prefer canary seed, as well as various small grass and weed seeds (fresh and sprouted), a fine-grade insectivorous mixture (there are various reliable commercial brands on the market), white worms, cut-up mealworms, fruit flies, green flies and small maggots. During the breeding season animal protein is essential.

Dusky Twin-spot   *Euschistospiza (or Hypargos) cinereovinacea*

DESCRIPTION: Head, breast, upperparts, and wings dark gray; flanks and uppertail coverts deep red; the flanks have a vague drop-design. Breast black with many white spots (drops). Rest of body black. Eyes red-brown with a red periophthalmic ring, beak black, legs gray-brown. The female is somewhat duller and the drops on the plumage are indistinct. Young birds are gray-brown. The song is similar to that of Dybowski's Twin-spot. Length: five inches (12 cm.).

DISTRIBUTION AND HABITAT: Southwestern Uganda, on the west side of Lake Tanganyika, and in central Angola. Often high in the mountains (6,000 feet and more) in pairs or (sometimes) in small flocks; also along the edges of forests, in savannas and grassland, close to water. They look for nourishment in bushes and on the ground.

CAPTIVITY: This is a bird for the expert aviculturist. The species must be housed in a well-planted indoor aviary with a constant temperature of 73° F (23° C). They are only allowed in outdoor facilities during really warm spring and summer weather. The birds were first imported in Europe in 1963, and two years later breeding successes were established. The birds are extremely nervous, and won't tolerate disturbances during the breeding season. Pairs like half-open nest boxes and bunches of heather, but will also breed in dense bushes, where they construct round nests from plant fibers, grass, wool, moss, small feathers and little roots.

FOOD: See DYBOWSKI'S TWIN-SPOT.

Genus *Hypargos* (Twin-spots)

Pink-throated Twin-spot   *Hypargos margaritatus*

DESCRIPTION: Looks very much like the Dusky Twin-spot, only the red is much sharper. It is, therefore, not surprising that various taxonomists regard the previous species as a member of this genus. Length: five inches (13 cm.).

DISTRIBUTION AND HABITAT: Southeast Africa; in woodland, along the edges of forests, and quiet roads, in pastures and close to small villages. They feed primarily on the ground.

CAPTIVITY: This excellent vitrine and indoor aviary bird must be acclimatized with the utmost care. Only well-planted housing facilities, with a temperature of at least 50° F (10° C), are appropriate. For further details see DUSKY TWIN-SPOT.

FOOD: See DYBOWSKI'S TWIN-SPOT.

Peter's Twin-spot *Hypargos niveoguttatus*

DESCRIPTION: Forehead and crown gray-brown; face, shoulders, rump and uppertail coverts red. Tail red with black on the tip. Belly and undertail coverts black. Flanks black with large white spots. Eyes brown (with a light gray-blue periophthalmic ring), beak blue-gray, legs dark gray. The female has a brownish head, and a red throat and breast; the underside is light brown-gray with little white spots. The young are much grayer than the female and miss all the white spots. Both sexes have a pleasant song, but the female's is much softer and sometimes somewhat screeching. Length: five inches (13 cm.).

DISTRIBUTION AND HABITAT: East Africa. The birds can be found in dense bushes, in forests and woods, close to water. They operate in pairs and even occur close to human settlements. Their nests are built in bushes or on the ground.

CAPTIVITY: This friendly bird, both to keeper and other small birds, must be carefully acclimatized at a temperature of 77° F (25° C). After approximately six weeks the temperature may be dropped to about 68° F (20° C). The birds don't withstand cold nights, and sleeping boxes must therefore be provided year 'round. During fall and winter they are best housed indoors (at room temperature). When their facilities are well-planted, breeding successes are very possible; they wouldn't tolerate disturbances, however. Their free-standing round nests are constructed in a bush or in a half-open nest box. During the breeding season a pair might sometimes be aggressive toward other finches.

FOOD: See PINK-THROATED TWIN-SPOT and MELBA FINCH. A variety of small insects (white worms, cut-up mealworms, small maggots, fruit flies, ant pupae, and a fine-grade commercial insectivorous mixture) is essential throughout the year, but especially during the breeding season.

Genus *Lagonosticta* (Fire Finches)

African Fire Finch *Lagonosticta rubricata*

DESCRIPTION: Dark red. Crown, back, and wings brownish-red to grayish-brown. Along the bend of the wing some little white spots. Yellowish periophthalmic ring. Eyes light brown, beak grayish with a reddish sheen (especially the lower mandible), legs gray-blue. The female is duller and more

148

light red to yellow in coloration, especially on throat, breast and belly. Young birds are grayish with red upper-tail coverts. Both sexes have a nice, clear song. During courtship the cock spreads his tail like a Chinese fan, while singing almost constantly. Length: four inches (11 cm.).

DISTRIBUTION AND HABITAT: Africa, south of the Sahara, except in the extremely southern regions. Their habitat is savannas, grassland, along forest edges, in neglected agricultural areas and similar places. The species lives close to the ground, in dense, thorny bushes, where it searches for small insects and various small seeds. The nest is usually built in thorny bushes, or in thick grassy clumps.

CAPTIVITY: Especially well-suited for indoor aviaries. Imported birds must be acclimatized at a temperature of approximately 68° F (20° C). Breeding successes are very possible (see Red-billed Fire Finch). The female lays three to five eggs, often six, which are hatched in about two weeks (sometimes less—eleven days minimum). A pair usually uses a nesting box, although they sometimes build a bullet-shaped nest in a dense bush close to the ground. In order to promote successful breeding, both parents and later their young will need an ample supply of insects. The species is rather peaceful toward other birds.

FOOD: See RED-BILLED FIRE FINCH.

Brown Fire Finch   *Lagonosticta nitidula*

DESCRIPTION: Gray-brown. Face and breast red; the latter with little white spots. Eyes brown, beak red, legs gray-brown. The female has less red. Young birds lack the white spots and still have a black bill; their general plumage is brownish. Length: four inches (11 cm.).

DISTRIBUTION AND HABITAT: Angola, the southern parts of Zaire, Zambia and the northern regions of Rhodesia; in grass and reeds. They build their nests in dense bushes, close to the ground; but also occupy old finch nests.

CAPTIVITY: In recent years, irregularly available in the trade. They are excellent birds for well-planted indoor aviaries. They breed in half-open nest boxes as well as in free-standing nests in thick bushes. It sometimes happens that a pair of Brown Fire Finches take over nests of other birds, but in general, they are very peaceful and won't present any problems if we supply them with various old finch nests and enough half-open nesting boxes.

FOOD: See RED-BILLED FIRE FINCH. Experience has taught that this species seldom accepts cut-up mealworms but rather feeds on ant pupae and white worms.

Black-faced Fire Finch *Lagonosticta larvata*

DESCRIPTION: Black face and throat; forehead, crown and neck gray-brown; uppertail coverts and center tail feathers deep red; undertail coverts dark gray. The rest of the body is brownish wine-red, with little white spots on the breast. Eyes dark brown with a blue periophthalmic ring, beak steel blue, legs dark brown. There is a subspecies which has a black throat and more gray on back and wings: the Black-throated Fire Finch (*L. l. nigricollis*). Females are duller and have a grayish-yellow throat and cheeks; back and crown are brown-gray. Young resemble the female. Length: four inches (11 cm.).

DISTRIBUTION AND HABITAT: Savasnna belt from Gambia to Ethiopia and the northern parts of Uganda; in grassland and bamboo. There are four subspecies in northwestern Africa, of which the Vinaceous Fire Finch (*L. l. vinacea*) is by far the best known. They like to use canary nest boxes which we have to place in dense, low bushes. All species build a cone-shaped, free-standing nest from plant fibers, moss and small feathers. It is primarily the female who is in the "building trade"; although the male brings practically all the materials, he seldom is "constructive." It takes the birds three to five days to complete their nest.

CAPTIVITY: This beautiful species is extremely suitable for indoor facilities. It becomes friendly toward keeper and other small finches in no time at all. Often a low, free-standing nest in a dense bush is built of grass, wool, moss, plant fibers, hay, small feathers, etc. They also like to use canary nests and various nest boxes. The three or four eggs hatch in 11 days; both parents take turns in brooding, but at night they spend it cozily together on the nest. When the young are approximately 19 days old they leave the nest but will be nourished for yet another week. After still another week we must separate them from their parents. Don't check nests, eggs or young while the parents are on or near the nest as they are very susceptible to disturbances and might abandon their offspring.

FOOD: See RED-BILLED FIRE FINCH. Insects as well as various commercial fine-grade softbill mixtures, soaked and germinated seed and seeding grasses are absolutely essential both in and out of the breeding season.

Black-breasted Fire Finch *Lagonosticta rufopicta*

DESCRIPTION: Very similar to the Red-billed Fire Finch, only the red in the male is less intensive. Primaries are much lighter; crown, neck, shoulders and back brown with a yellowish sheen. On the breast small white bars. The female has red underparts and cheeks; the rest of the body is brownish-gray. Length: four inches (10 cm.).

DISTRIBUTION AND HABITAT: Savanna belt from Gambia to Ethiopia and northern Uganda; in savannas, bushes, close to villages and in large gardens and parks.

CAPTIVITY: As the above species. The female lays three to five eggs (in the wild up to seven), which are incubated by both parents. The young hatch after 10-11 days, and leave the nest when approximately 17 days old.

FOOD: As the BLACK-FACED FIRE FINCH; small insects are essential throughout the year, but especially during the breeding season.

Jameson's Fire Finch *Lagonosticta rhodopreia*

DESCRIPTION: Similar to the African Fire Finch, but much lighter. The subspecies *L. r. jamesoni* or Red-headed Jameson's Finch, has a much brighter red back and head. The *L. rhodopareia* has brownish upperparts and a brown head. Length: four inches (11 cm.).

DISTRIBUTION AND HABITAT: From southern Africa, East Africa to Ethiopia, and from Angola to Zaire. It is a typical savanna-bird, where it searches for small seeds and insects on the ground, in low, dense bushes or in grass clumps. The bullet-shaped nest is built in thorny bushes.

CAPTIVITY: This bird is available only occasionally. It is an excellent indoor aviary bird; as it likes roomy well-planted facilities, cages are unsuitable. For more details see RED-BILLED FIRE FINCH.

FOOD: Without animal protein, breeding results will be rare. This species needs small insects (white worms, cut-up mealworms, ant pupae, small maggots, etc.) throughout the year, but especially during the breeding and rearing period.

Red-billed Fire Finch *Lagonosticta senegala*

DESCRIPTION: Crimson; darker, sometimes reddish-brown on back and wings. All primaries have light edges. Rump, flanks, cheeks, and throat light red. Belly whitish with a red sheen. Tail brownish-red to dark red. Near the bend of the wing and on the breast tiny white spots. Eyes reddish brown with a small yellow periophthalmic ring, beak light red, legs light brown. The female is brownish-gray with some white spots on the side of the breast; her mask is crimson. There is a reddish sheen on the breast. Tail dark brown. Young birds are fully colored after approximately five months; initially they are very similar to the female, although young males show the small white spots at an early age. Length: four inches (9 cm.).

DISTRIBUTION AND HABITAT: From Senegal to the Red Sea, and from East Africa to South Africa, north and south of the Kalahari Desert to the Atlantic Ocean; in grassland, savannas, and large gardens and parks; always near human habitation. The species is parasitized by the Senegal Combassou (*Vidua chalybeata*).

CAPTIVITY: This rather shy bird builds its nest of hair, wool, moss, leaves, sisal, blades of grass, stems of rootlets, and other fibers; the lining is made from small feathers. Both sexes are in the "building trade." The nest is quite roughly constructed and bullet-shaped. They will also use nesting boxes, old weaver and finch nests, etc., and will even build a nest under the eaves. In an indoor aviary they will also breed during the winter months, but then we should not allow them to continue breeding in the summer. The hatching period is about 12 days; the three to five, sometimes six, young leave the nest after approximately 18 days, but they will still be fed by their parents for another 18-20 days. The hens are generally weaker than the cocks, so that the aviculturist should keep an eye out for egg binding. It is certainly best to wait a year after buying a pair before allowing them to breed so that all this unpleasantness is avoided. In the wild as well as in captivity, the birds prefer to stay on the ground, where they search for small insects, spiders, grass and weed seeds.

Birds that are not yet acclimatized find it difficult to tolerate drafts and cold. They fare best at an even temperature of 68° F (20° C). During the fall and winter I prefer to house my birds inside in roomy cages or indoor aviaries at room temperature. During the breeding season the male's display is very interesting to watch as he dances in front of his bride with a blade of grass or sometimes a small feather in his beak. Copulation usually takes place on the ground; prior to this act, the male pecks his partner gently in the neck feathers; she answers by moving her tail from right to left. A nest box placed in a little thicket will be accepted sooner than one that is hung against one of the walls of the aviary. Never allow more than three broods per season, which runs from April to the middle of September; later broods must be discouraged.

FOOD: All small millet varieties, spray millet, a good commercial seed mix, grass and weed seeds (fresh, sprouted and germinated), greens (lettuce, chickweed, spinach, dandelion, etc.), small insects (white worms, daphnias, cut-up mealworms, small maggots, spiders, ant pupae), egg and rearing food for finches, various commercial fine-grade softbill mixtures, cuttle bone, vitamins and minerals.

OTHER NAME: Common Fire Finch.

Black-bellied Waxbill   *Lagonosticta rara*

DESCRIPTION: Dark red; underparts, undertail coverts, and tail black. Wings brownish. Eyes brown, beak black, lower mandible with red on the sides, legs brown. The female is brownish, as are the young. The male has a melodious song, which he seldom performs, however. Length: four inches (11 cm.).

DISTRIBUTION AND HABITAT: From Nigeria to Uganda and Sierra Leone. Lives primarily on the ground. Builds its nest in thorny bushes as well as under the cane roofs.

CAPTIVITY: Infrequently imported bird, which is, especially in the beginning, extremely shy and even with excellent care and management never becomes totally familiar with its keeper or other birds. Therefore only suitable for large, well-planted aviaries. May also be housed outdoors in our warmer areas. It will come to breeding if enough half-open nesting boxes are made available. It often happens, however, that the parents neglect their young, even if enough animal protein is provided.

FOOD: See RED-BILLED FIRE FINCH.

Genus *Lonchura* (Mannikins and Munias)

Dusky Munia   *Lonchura fuscans*

DESCRIPTION: Similar to the Java Munia; the lower mandible and legs, however, are blue-gray. Length: four inches (11 cm.).

DISTRIBUTION AND HABITAT: Borneo (Indonesia); in grassland and savannas, rice fields, gardens and parks, forests, along roads, near water and villages. Nests high in thick trees and under tiles of local huts and houses.

CAPTIVITY: This species is seldom imported. It remains shy for a long time, and breeds only rarely. Needs a well-planted, roomy aviary. Cross-breedings with Bengalese are possible, and their young are fertile. It is a pleasant and quiet bird that really deserves much more attention from the more serious aviculturist!

FOOD: See SHARP-TAILED MUNIA.

Chestnut-breasted Finch   *Lonchura castaneothorax*

DESCRIPTION: Head grayish-brown with light markings; dark brown mantle and wings. Yellowish rump and uppertail coverts. Yellowish tail. Throat, chin and face blackish-brown. Breast chestnut; lower parts black. Underparts and undertail coverts pure white. Eyes brown, beak grayish-blue, legs gray-brown. The sexes are alike, although females are somewhat duller, especially on flanks and head. Length: four inches (11 cm.).

DISTRIBUTION AND HABITAT: Tropical North and East Australia, along the coast (near Sydney) in two subspecies. Also in Papua New Guinea and Vulcan Island. Introduced into New Caledonia, Society Islands, and Tahiti. Their habitat is grassland, cane fields, reed beds, and along the coastal districts of northern Australia, where they live in sometimes large flocks. They often destroy whole cereal crops.

CAPTIVITY: Rarely available in the trade, although various European aviculturists are occasionally breeding this amicable bird in well-planted (reeds!), large, outdoor aviaries with a variety of nesting boxes. Before the

Lonchura malacca.

Lonchura malacca atricapilla.

Red-billed Fire Finch cock *(Lagonostica senegala).*

Photo by author

154

breeding starts, the male dances in front of his mate, drawing himself up to his full height, while hopping up and down on his branch or perch. This species is excellent for the beginner, but it must be said that they practically never breed. There have been some successes in cross-breeding them with several mannikins, Striated Munia, Indian Silverbill, Masked Grassfinch, and Zebra Finch. They are pleasant, tolerant birds that never get into arguments and bear up quite well in most circumstances. They also need fresh bath water daily, and nail care—like all the other *Lonchura* species! The female lays four to six eggs; the incubation time is approximately two weeks. The young leave the nest after about 21 days. The first few evenings the male delegates his youngsters back to the parental nest where the whole family spends the night. After about a month the young are independent.

FOOD: Small and medium size millets, spray millet, oats, grass and weed seeds, thistle seed, and buckwheat (fresh, sprouted and germinated). Greens (lettuce, chickweed, dandelion, spinach, *etc.*), apple, pear and oranges. Throughout the year but especially during the breeding and rearing period, ant pupae, cut-up mealworms, white worms, small maggots, egg and rearing food for finches, and milk- or water-soaked white bread, cuttle bone, minerals and vitamins.

Great-billed Mannikin *Lonchura grandis*

DESCRIPTION: Black; wings and back red-brownish. Eyes brown-red, beak light gray, legs gray. Length: five inches (12 cm.).

DISTRIBUTION AND HABITAT: Southeastern and northern New Guinea; primarily a swamp bird, although sometimes found in grassland. They construct their nest from grass and other plant fibers, usually in grassy clumps, but also in trees or bushes.

CAPTIVITY: This species is seldom imported; I saw the first captive birds in Switzerland in 1970. Care and management are similar to the other *Lonchura* species.

Tri-Colored Munia *Lonchura malacca.* See *L. m. atricapilla*

DESCRIPTION: Head, neck, nape, throat and partly the breast black; flanks and breast white; underparts and undertail coverts black. Wing, back and tail brown. Eyes dark brown, beak light blue-gray, legs grayish-black. The white in the female is not as clear as in the male. Length: five inches (12 cm.).

DISTRIBUTION AND HABITAT: India and Sri Lanka, through southeastern Asia, Sumatra, Taiwan, the Philippines, Sulawesi (formerly Celebes), and Java (Indonesia); in grassland and cultivated areas, in sometimes large flocks.

CAPTIVITY: This extremely strong and lively bird is excellent for the beginner.

155

It is, however, far from easy to breed, but in quiet, large and well-planted (reeds, corn, grass, dense bushes) garden aviaries it sometimes will use the deserted nests of canaries or other finches, and raise a family. We should leave a few flagstones on the aviary floor to act as manicurists (sorry, pedicurists!), and keep their nails in shape. The birds will not tolerate inspections during the breeding cycle. Supply them with perches located high in the aviary, and offer them plenty of insects. The female lays three to five eggs; incubation time: 13 days. The young leave the nest after approximately 20 days, but are fed by their parents for another two or three weeks. After six months the young are fully colored.

FOOD: Like the SPICE FINCH. Provide them with a variety of insects, cuttle bone, weed and grass seeds, egg and rearing food for finches, greens, and stale bread soaked in milk or water.

OTHER NAME: Chestnut Munia, Tri-colored Nun.

Yellow-tailed Finch   *Lonchura flaviprymna*

DESCRIPTION: Yellow back, reddish-brown breast, and brownish-yellow underparts. Throat white, crown grayish-blue. Eyes dark brown, beak gray-blue, legs dark grayish-blue. Length: four inches (11 cm.).

DISTRIBUTION AND HABITAT: Northwestern Australia and Northern Territory; in grassland, swamps and reedy margins, often in the company of the Chestnut-breasted Finch; cross-breedings in the wild between those two species are possible. For more details see the TRI-COLORED MUNIA.

CAPTIVITY: These birds are somewhat easier to breed when three or more pairs are placed in a large, well-planted garden aviary. The female lays five or six eggs.

FOOD: See SPICE FINCH and TRI-COLORED MUNIA.

Bengalese   *Lonchura striata* var. *domestica*

DESCRIPTION: This species, which is not found in the wild, occurs in various shades of brown and white, and there are even some varieties that have a little crest.

CAPTIVITY: A gentle, friendly disposition and an aptitude for breeding and raising families—even in small spaces—has given this species the name Society Finch. These characteristics also have lent the Bengalese its reputation as an excellent foster parent for more temperamental species.

Eggs from other birds, especially Australian Grass Finches, can be given for adoption to Society Finches to reduce the risk of mishap. It doesn't matter if the eggs have been brooded by the original parents for awhile; in fact, Bengalese will not be upset if the eggs they are brooding hatch after they have been in their care for only, say, five or six days.

Lonchura flaviprymna.

A chocoalate self Bengalese.

Photo by author

157

Even young hatchlings abandoned by their true parents can be entrusted to Bengalese for further care if the finches have been raising young at more or less the same age and stage of development.

Foster nestlings should be returned to their natural parents once they reach adulthood; otherwise, these young birds will want to stay near Society Finches and won't associate with their own kind. Such imprinting should be prevented if one intends to breed the birds later.

The use of Society Finches as foster parents has engendered a good deal of controversy, however, especially with regard to Australian grass finches such as Gouldians. In *The Care and Breeding of Seed-eating Birds* (see BIBLIOGRAPHY), Mr. J. Trollope states: "The Gouldian Finch is the main species to be reared by this method. Some aviculturists maintain this is the reason for infertility sometimes occurring in some strains of Gouldian Finches. They also point out the evils of imprinting; that is, Gouldians reared by Bengalese 'think' they are Bengalese and, when of breeding age, fail to respond to the reproductive behavior of other Gouldians. Others say this is not a problem and there is no evidence to suggest such imprinting occurs."

Nevertheless, based on their world fame as foster parents, any serious bird fancier interested in rearing finches should have at least two or three pair of Bengalese.

When purchasing a pair of Society Finches, however, one must be sure the sales contract permits an exchange if they turn out to be an ineffective couple. Spelling out the exact guarantee is good business for both buyer and seller.

These measures are necessary because it's hard to sex Bengalese. Only the song of the male—a rather attractive, soft rasp—can help sex the birds successfully, but there is no similar test for females.

To further confound the breeder, two females, when placed together, act like a breeding pair. They build a nest, lay eggs—infertile ones, of course—and take turns brooding. Even two males together can act like a "pair." They don't sing, but build empty nests with brooding chambers, sitting for days on the empty nest as if they were brooding. Although demand is high for these birds, if you pick a reliable breeder and have a little luck, you can acquire real breeding pairs.

The Bengalese has, as stated, no real counterpart in the wild but was itself bred from the Sharp-tailed munia (*Lonchura acuticauda*) and the Striata munia (*Lonchura striata*). The American aviculturist, Mr. Allan Silver, believes the African Silverbill (*Lonchura cantans*) also was involved in the development of the Society Finch.

Different varieties were bred during its period of domestication (which can be traced back to about 1700), until the Bengalese finally became a very popular ornamental bird. It came to Europe quite late, getting to England in 1860, to Germany in 1872, to Holland in 1874; and to the United States between 1890 and 1895 (althouth it didn't become popular until around 1950).

Society Finches are good breeders and are suitable both as aviary and cage birds. They usually are quite passive and won't confront other birds in the aviary or cage. They will allow nesting material to be stolen from their nest box, even if they are in the midst of building or brooding. In fact, Bengalese let themselves be pushed around to the point of giving up their whole nest to other birds. Some individual Society Finches will stand up for their rights, but they are the exceptions.

In short, Bengalese need support from the hobbyist to breed successfully—not because the birds are unwilling, but because they don't get the chance. Therefore, these birds should be provided a breeding cage of adequate size or a spacious aviary.

Many aviculturists consistently get 15 to 20 young a year from a pair of Society Finches. Personally, I think this is overdoing things; one should not take advantage of the birds. Unless you intervene, they will continue to breed winter and summer. This is not advisable because the female would be fatally weakened by egg binding and general exhaustion. It is best not to allow more than three broods per season.

Select a breeding time for them, either in spring or summer, that fits your schedule. The winter months also can be used if you supply a spacious, well-lit indoor aviary room or large breeding cage.

The normal brooding period for Bengalese is 20-21 days. After another 20 days, the young are ready to leave the nest, but the parents continue to feed them for some time. After about 40 days, when the young are no longer being fed by their parents, they can be removed and placed in a large box cage. Young birds should not be used for breeding until they are at least one year old.

Society Finches occur, as stated already, in various brownish and white colors; some have a little crest. If a breeder prefers a particular color, he will need to continue breeding just that particular color three to five times. Or, to keep the birds' lineage pure (homozygous) as possible, and in lieu of keeping well-organized records, the young could be ringed eight to ten days after they have emerged from the eggs. However, these birds are excellent for all kinds of cross-breedings; the resultant hybrids often win high awards at European bird shows.

Again, the breeding itself does not usually pose many problems. In a well-planted aviary or in a box cage, one can achieve very satisfactory results. Do not disturb the breeding birds, however, even if they are known as birds that allow regular nest inspection. Even Society Finches find peace a necessary condition.

Supply the birds with large nest boxes (half-open; 10″ × 10″ × 10″; 25 × 25 × 25 cm.) and ample nesting material (coconut fibers and grass, for example); remember, some finches will allow other, more aggressive birds to take an unfair share of these materials.

Bengalese tend to have fast-growing nails, so some flagstones should be

159

put in the aviary to serve as nail files. Special attention should be given to perches, since they are so important to foot health. They should be made of good hardwood such as oak or beech, and should not be too thin. A diameter of 1" to 1½" is suitable, allowing the bird to clasp its foot around the perch comfortably.

Sandpaper perch covers—sleeves that fit over the perches—are widely known and, provided they are used properly, could aid in keeping claws trimmed. Don't cover all the perches, however, as constant resting on perches covered with sandpaper might aggravate the feet. At least a few naked perches are necessary to prevent sores.

These birds also require fresh bathing water daily, as well as a varied tropical seed mix and a quickly replenished supply of insects.

FOOD: Millet varieties, canary grass seed, rape seed, flax, poppyseed, hulled oats or oat groats, apple (raw), bread (stale, milk or water-soaked), cracker meal, peanuts (cracked), spinach, cracked sunflower seed, weed seeds and wheat germ. During the breeding season: egg food for finches, fine-grade softbill meal, gentles (cleaned larva of the blowfly or bluebottle fly), insectivorous food, small flies (two to four per bird; four to six during the breeding season), small cut-up mealworms, spiders, ant pupae, white worms, and sprouted seeds. On a daily basis (in order of importance): water, vitamins, minerals, cuttle bone, crushed oyster shell, baked chicken eggshells, mineral grit and spray millet.

OTHER NAME: Society Finch.

Java Munia   *Lonchura leucogastroides*

DESCRIPTION: Crown, breast and throat black; belly white, blackish toward the tail. Cheeks, wings and back brown. There is a vague stripe-design on the wing. Undertail coverts usually light brown. Eyes brownish-red, upper mandible black, lower mandible gray, legs gray-brown. The sexes are alike, but the male has a pleasant chirping song. Length: four inches (11 cm.).

DISTRIBUTION AND HABITAT: Java and Sunda Islands; in high grass, reeds, and thick bushes, but also along the edges of forests, in agricultural developments, gardens and parks, and along roads. Their main diet consists of rice, but during the breeding season various small insects are caught and fed to the young.

CAPTIVITY: A friendly, quiet bird, suitable for large cages, vitrines and aviaries. A pair usually builds a nest in a thick bush near the ground, although now and again half-open nesting boxes are used as well.

FOOD: See BENGALESE.

160

Spice Finch *Lonchura punctulata*

DESCRIPTION: Head, throat and neck chocolate brown; back and wings dark brown; rump light brown; breast and flanks white; the feathers have brown edges (scaly); underparts light brown, and white on the abdomen. Tail brown, uppertail coverts dark brown. The sexes are alike but the male's beak is somewhat thicker and heavier; the head is larger and broader. The male also stands out because of the very soft song, with the head held high and puffed throat feathers. It is a pity that you can hardly hear anything of his song! Young birds don't have the scaly appearance. Eyes dark brown, beak steel grayish-black, legs gray-brown. Length: four inches (11 cm.).

DISTRIBUTION AND HABITAT: In various subspecies in India, Sri Lanka, southeastern Asia, south China, Taiwan and Hainan, through Greater and Lesser Sundas (except Borneo) to Sulawesi (formerly Celebes) and the Philippines; introduced into Australia (1942). Their habitat is grassland, parks and gardens, rice paddies, and along the edges of forests. Usually near people. Feed on rice, grass and weed seeds, and during the rearing time, various small insects.

CAPTIVITY: This bird is practically always available in the trade. It is modest in its demands and is suitable for garden and large indoor aviaries. In the winter it must be housed indoors in a frost-free area, but this doesn't imply that this species cannot tolerate temperate zones. Experience has shown that, if the birds are given an outside aviary, with a sturdily build night enclosure (containing felt-lined nest boxes, which also serve as sleeping places), they can spend the winter outdoors. A pair builds a rather large, round nest in a thick bush; they seldom use nesting boxes. The female lays three to five eggs, sometimes seven to ten. For more details, see the various Silverbills. Cross-breedings are possible with Bengalese, Silverbill, Java Sparrow, and various Munias. Hens have a tendency to suffer from egg binding, so a careful control is essential.

FOOD: We can keep the birds in excellent health by giving them a variety of insects throughout the year, as well as weed seeds and a tropical seed mix, some cod liver oil, and stale bread soaked in milk or water. For more nutritional information see BENGALESE.

OTHER NAME: Nutmeg Mannikin.

Sclater's Mannikin *Lonchura spectabilis*

DESCRIPTION: Primarily black, except for the reddish, chocolate-brown wings and back. Uppertail coverts and tail with yellowish-brown feather edges; underparts white with some yellowish or brownish sheen. Eyes dark reddish-brown, beak gray, legs dark gray. The sexes are alike; the male sings an almost inaudible song, similar to that of the Spice Finch. When the birds

161

detect danger they sound a high pitched "geeeec, geeeec"-call. Length: four inches (10 cm.).

DISTRIBUTION AND HABITAT: Eastern parts of New Guinea, the islands of the Bismarck Archipelago, and New Britain. The birds operate in small groups, also during the breeding season. They feed on grass and weed seeds. The nests are constructed in dense bushes, in high grass clumps or in reeds.

CAPTIVITY: Since 1970, irregularly available in the trade. Excellent for vitrines and large cages, but, obviously, best for aviaries. They are friendly toward their own kind and other small finches. Pairs often build sleeping nests, even outside the breeding season. For more details regarding breeding, care and management see CHESTNUT-BREASTED FINCH.

FOOD: See CHESTNUT-BREASTED FINCH.

Black-throated Munia   *Lonchura malacca ferruginosa*

DESCRIPTION: Similar to the Black-headed Munia; underparts white. This white color doesn't run further than the neck. Length: four inches (11 cm.).

DISTRIBUTION AND HABITAT: Java and Bali; in reed and tall grass. They build their nests in grass clumps. Often a pest in rice paddies, to the great annoyance of the farmers. Sometimes in surprisingly large flocks of hundreds of birds.

CAPTIVITY: An excellent bird for the beginner. The species, however, must be housed in a roomy aviary, as they become sick in small quarters. They are friendly toward their own kind as well as to other small finches. A pair regularly comes to breed, especially if it has company. Excellent results are achieved when three or more pairs are housed in the same aviary. Thick plantings (reed, tall grass, thick bushes, etc.) are necessary. The female lays three to five eggs which hatch after 13 days. The young leave the nest after about 24 days, but will return to their "cradle" for the night for at least another ten days. After six weeks the young are independent, and after six months look like their parents.

FOOD: See BENGALESE.

Sharp-tailed Munia   *Lonchura striata acuticauda*

DESCRIPTION: Head, throat, back and wings chocolate-brown; cheeks, neck, flanks and breast lighter. The neck has a vague bar design. Rump grayish-white, with little brown bars; underparts white. Eyes reddish-brown, upper mandible black, lower mandible light blue-gray. The sexes are alike, but the male has a soft song, similar to that of the Society Finch. Length: five inches (12 cm.).

162

DISTRIBUTION AND HABITAT: Sri Lanka and India. There are various subspecies of which, obviously, the Striata Munia, White-rumped Mannikin or White-backed Munia (*Lonchura striata striata*) is by far the most important one for the trade. This *striata*-species lives in the Himalayas, India, Sri Lanka, southern China, Taiwan, Banka Island, the Andamans and Nicobars. This bird is probably the wild ancestor of the Society Finch, together with the Sharp-tailed Munia. All the *striata*-subspecies have their habitat in grass and reed, gardens, parks, orchards, along roads and sometimes even close to human settlements. They are also found along the edges of forests and in agricultural areas; sometimes in large flocks in the rice paddies, where they are often a pest!

CAPTIVITY: The Sharp-tailed Munia is friendly, suitable for cages, vitrines and aviaries. When there are thick plantings or various nesting boxes, pairs often breed. The male dances around his future bride with ruffled feathers. The female lays four to six eggs; both sexes brood the eggs, which hatch after approximately 14 days. After about 21 days the young leave their "cradle," but return for the night to the parental nest. The young are independent after about two weeks, but they can't be put to breeding till they are at least 11-12 months old.

FOOD: All varieties of millets, fresh as well as germinated or soaked (especially in the breeding season). A rich variety of greens is absolutely necessary, as well as grass and weed seeds; for more details see SOCIETY FINCH.

OTHER NAME: Striated Munia.

Pictorella Finch *Lonchura pectoralis*

DESCRIPTION: Crown, neck, back, and wings grayish-green; rump somewhat lighter; cheeks and throat dark blue. An orange-brown stripe from above the eye to cheeks, neck and throat. Breast white with a black scallop-design; along the flanks some black-brownish scalloping with white edges; the same along the black tail-feathers. The top-side of the tail-feathers is grayish. Primaries black with gray-brown edges; the greater wing coverts with white tips and black edges. The female has a brown-grayish back; the stripe above the eye is brown. Length: five inches (12 cm.).

DISTRIBUTION AND HABITAT: Northwestern Australia and Northern Territory; in grassland and savannas, usually in extremely dry country. The nest is built low between grass clumps. The species forages primarily on the ground, in small groups.

CAPTIVITY: Rather rare in aviculture. The bird is very friendly toward its keeper as well as toward other small birds. The mating dances of the male are performed on the ground; he dances around his future bride while bobbing his head and sometimes touching the female's bill, or picking in the sand. The

163

wings are carried low and the tail goes from right to left. The half-open nesting boxes must be partially filled with nesting materials. Hang those boxes low, near the ground (between 30″ and 40″; 70-100 cm.), in dense bushes. It is advisable to have corn, reed, high grass, and bushes as main plantings in the aviary. The female lays four or five eggs, which will be hatched—primarily by the female—in about 13 days. The young leave the nest after 22 days but will be foraged-for by both parents for another week to 10 days. After about 40 days the young are fully capable of looking after themselves.

Newly imported birds must be acclimatized with care at a temperature of about 77° F (25° C). Birds born in captivity are hardy but must be placed indoors when the temperature drops below 65° F (18° C).

FOOD: Similar to all the other *Lonchura*-species from Australia, i.e., grass and weed seed, millets, white seed, poppyseed, hemp (if available), egg and rearing food for finches, greens (see BENGALESE), white bread soaked in water or milk, cuttle bone, grit, charcoal, cut-up mealworms, ant pupae, small spiders, green flies, and small maggots.

OTHER NAME: Pectoral Finch or Pectoral Mannikin.

White-headed Munia   *Lonchura maja*

DESCRIPTION: White head; upperparts chestnut; underparts black. Sexes are alike, but sometimes the male's head is brighter. Eyes brown, beak dark blue-gray, legs grayish-black. Length: four inches (11 cm.).

DISTRIBUTION AND HABITAT: Malay Peninsula, Sumatra, Simalur, Nias, Java, and Bali (Indonesia); in grassland, sometimes in enormous flocks. This species construct their nests in grass clumps; they are small and made from grass and vegetable fibers.

CAPTIVITY: These birds are very much in demand around the world. Although the breeding results from these birds are only average, it is eventually possible that a pair will breed if the cage is in a very quiet and restful spot. There is a better chance of breeding if a male is mated with a Society Finch. Once they start breeding, you can expect the four or five young in about 12 days; after 25-30 days, they leave the nest but still take food from the parents for awhile. Their nails grow quite long (as is the case with all *Lonchura*-species) and should be carefully trimmed twice a year; a job that is far from easy, but necessary. The birds must have fresh bathwater daily. This species can grow rather old; I have seen birds of 18 and 20 years old!

FOOD: See BENGALESE.

OTHER NAMES: White-headed Mannikin and White-headed Nun.

Black-headed Munia   *Lonchura malacca atricapilla*

DESCRIPTION: Head, upper breast, center of belly, and undertail coverts

Lonchura maja.

Mandingoa nitidula.

Neochmia phaëton.

black. Rest of upperparts chestnut brown; reddish on tail coverts and tail. White lower breast and flanks. The sexes are alike. Eyes brown, beak blue-gray, legs dark blue-gray. Length: five inches (12 cm.).

DISTRIBUTION AND HABITAT: India and Sri Lanka, through southeastern Asia, Sumatra, Taiwan, the Philippines, Sulawesi (formerly Celebes), and Java (Indonesia); in grassland and cultivated areas; in sometimes large flocks.

CAPTIVITY: This bird is controlled by export regulations. It is extremely strong, lively, and excellent for the beginner. During the winter months house all munias in quarters with room temperature. Care and management are the same as for the SPICE FINCH.

FOOD: See BENGALESE.

OTHER NAMES: Tri-colored Mannikin; Black-headed Nun.

Genus *Mandingoa* (Green-backed Twin-spots)

Green-backed Twin-spot *Mandingoa nitidula*

DESCRIPTION: Red-orange face; deep olive-yellow uppertail coverts; some olive-yellow on throat, upper breast, and neck. Olive-green undertail coverts. Black underparts with white spots. Eyes brown, beak black with a red tip, legs brownish. The female is duller and has a paler orange on the face. Length: four inches (11 cm.).

DISTRIBUTION AND HABITAT: Mozambique. There are two subspecies, of which the Schlegel's Twin-spot (*M. n. schlegeli*) of West Africa has a bright red face and a reddish chin and breast. The Chubb's Twin-spot (*M. n. chubbi*) is from East Africa, with a red face and a golden-yellow chin and breast, often washed in orange. The species live in small groups along the edges of forests and in thickets. They feed mainly on the ground.

CAPTIVITY: Lively, hardy birds which feed mainly on the ground. A thickly planted aviary is necessary. They are friendly towards other birds, hence excellent for a community aviary. During the breeding season sometimes quarrelsome towards small finches. They use half-open breeding boxes in which the female lays four or five eggs. The young hatch on the 13th day and leave the nest 21 days later. The first few days, up to a week, they often spend the night in the parental nest. Recently imported birds must be housed inside with a temperature of approximately 77° F (25° C). During warm, sunny summers they may be housed in garden aviaries.

FOOD: Ant pupae must be available year round, as well as white worms and cut-up mealworms (see also MELBA FINCH). For more details see BENGALESE.

Genus *Neochmia* (Crimson Waxbills)

Crimson Waxbill *Neochmia phaeton*

DESCRIPTION: Red, with a grayish sheen on the upperparts. Wings anthracite with red edges. Little white spots on flank and breast. Underparts dark red, darker on the belly. Underside wings yellow. The female is grayish; cheeks and throat wine-red; rump and uppertail coverts red with black feather edges. Wings grayish-red with dark brown feather edges. Eyes light yellow-brown, beak red (lighter on the female) with white on the base, legs grayish-yellow. Length: five inches (12 cm.).

DISTRIBUTION AND HABITAT: North Australia, and in a small area in New Guinea; in grassland, reed and savannas. Sometimes in trees and bushes.

CAPTIVITY: Rarely seen in aviculture. Keep only one pair per housing facility as more birds tend to fight and seldom breed. When the temperature drops below 68° F (20° C), they must be housed indoors at room temperature. The species is very nervous while breeding, so very susceptible to disturbances. They like to take canary nests as their "maternity room"; place these nests in thick bushes. Supply plant fibers, soft feathers, moss, grass, wool and pieces of bark. For more details see DIAMOND FINCH.

FOOD: See BENGALESE. Extra niger seed and spray millet throughout the year are necessary.

Genus *Nesocharis* (Oliveback Finches)

White-collared Oliveback   *Nesocharis ansorgei*

DESCRIPTION: Upperparts black; white neck band (grayish in *shelleyi*) and gray-blue neck feathers (yellow in *shelleyi*). Breast green-yellow. Back, rump, uppertail coverts and wings olive-green (uppertail coverts and rump golden yellow in *shelleyi*). Tail black, belly grayish-blue, as are the undertail coverts. The female has a grayish-blue breast. Eyes and legs dark brown (the legs of *shelleyi* are light brown), beak black. Length: four inches (10 cm.). The *shelleyi* is approximately three inches (8 cm.).

DISTRIBUTION AND HABITAT: The nominate form lives in Northern Congo to Uganda; in grassland, and along forests, close to water. The subspecies *N. a. shelleyi* or Little Olive Waxbill comes from Fernando Po and Cameroon.

CAPTIVITY: Excellent for well-planted indoor aviaries with a high humidity (75%). Seldom imported. Offer old weaver and finch nests, as well as nesting boxes (see BENGALESE). They rarely come to breeding, however. The same applies to the other species: the Gray-headed Oliveback (*N. capistrata*) from Equatorial Africa, from Gambia to Congo, western Uganda and the southern parts of Sudan. For more details see MELBA FINCH.

FOOD: See MELBA FINCH.

Genus *Nigrita* (Negro Finches)

None of the four species were ever imported to the USA, and are of no importance to the trade:

White-breasted Negro-finch, *Nigrita fusconota,* from Fernando Po and the forests of Ghana, Angola and Uganda;

Chestnut-breasted Negro-finch, *Nigrita bicolor,* from Principé and Sierra Leone to Angola and Uganda;

Pale-fronted Negro-finch, *Nigrita luteifrons,* from Fernando Po and Nigeria to Angola and Uganda, and

Gray-breasted Negro-finch, *Nigrita canicapilla,* from Guinea to Angola, Tanganyika and the southern parts of Sudan.

The species of the following Genera are never or seldom imported and therefore of little importance to aviculture:

Genus *Parmoptila*—Antpeckers; Woodhouse's Antpecker (*P. woodhousei*), from Equatorial Africa from Angola to Ghana and Uganda.

Genus *Pyrenestes*—Seed-crackers: Crimson Seed-cracker (*P. sanguineus*), from Gambia to the Ivory Coast; Black-bellied Seed-cracker (*P. ostrinus*), from the Ivory Coast to Angola, Uganda, and Zambia; Lesser Seed-cracker (*P. minor*), from eastern Tanganyika to northern Mozambique.

Genus *Spermophaga*—Blue-bills: Grant's Bluebill (*S poliogenys*), from Congo and Bwamba (Uganda); Common Bluebill (*S. haematina*), from Gambia to Congo and Angola; and Red-headed Bluebill (*S. ruficapilla*), from northern Angola to Uganda and Kenya.

Genus *Odontospiza* (Gray-headed Silverbills)

Gray-headed Silverbill *Odontospiza [Lonchura] caniceps*

DESCRIPTION: Head gray; cheeks and throat are covered with small white spots. Mantle and underparts pinkish-light-brown; rump and uppertail coverts white; wing coverts gray; tail and wings black. Sexes are alike, although the male is slightly richer in coloring and has larger white spots. Eyes brown, beak gray-blue, legs dark gray. Length: four inches (11 cm.).

DISTRIBUTION AND HABITAT: West and central Africa; in four subspecies. They live in savannas, farmland, and near villages, with nests often found under roofs and in the walls of huts or in low shrubs.

CAPTIVITY: These birds are easy breeders and can be placed in community aviaries as well as in large cages. The best breeding results, however, are obtained in aviaries where they can be by themselves. The aviary (or cage)

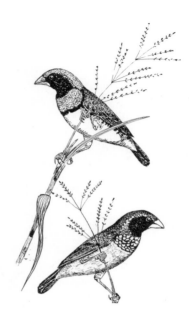

Above: *Lonchura castaneothorax;*
below: *Lonchura pectoralis.*

Black-bellied seed cracker *(Pyrenestes ostrinus).*   *Photo by author*

should be very quiet as they are susceptible to disturbance. Nest inspection therefore is taboo. The hen lays three or four eggs; both sexes incubate them for 12-13 days. The youngsters leave the nest 21 days later. Fifteen to twenty-one young from one pair in one season is not only possible but relatively common. Three broods per year, however, produce the best young, and also lower the risk of egg binding. Silverbills are extremely suitable foster parents for finches that don't require insects. They prefer greens, millet, and especially spray millet as a treat. They can be crossed with *L. malabarica, L. punctulata,* and *L. striata var. domestica,* among others. Offer nesting boxes of at least 6″ × 6″ × 8″ (15 × 15 × 20 cm.). They use a variety of building materials (plant fibers, wool, grass, hay, small feathers, etc.). House these birds inside (room temperature) during the fall and winter months.

FOOD: See BENGALESE.

Genus *Oreostrusthus* (Mountain Finches)

Crimson-side Mountain Finch   *Oreostrusthus fuliginosus*

DESCRIPTION: Throat, breast, flanks and uppertail coverts red; belly and undertail coverts brownish-black. Rest of body greenish gray-brown. Eyes brown, beak red, legs light pink. The female is lighter red and brown.

DISTRIBUTION AND HABITAT: New Guinea; high in the mountains (up to 10,000 feet; 3,000 meters). The bird is extremely shy, and therefore difficult to observe. They live in pairs.

CAPTIVITY: The bird was first imported in 1967 (Holland), and is since then irregularly available in Europe as well as in the USA. Care, management and feed are similar to the RED-HEADED PARROT FINCH.

Genus *Ortygospiza* (Quail Finches)

Common Quail Finch   *Ortygospiza atricollis*

DESCRIPTION: Upperparts mottled brown. Forehead and cheeks black. White chin and areas around the eyes. Throat black. Underparts grayish with black and white bars. Abdomen yellowish-brown. Eyes brown with usually a white periophthalmic ring and lores, beak red, legs brownish. The female is duller and has small brown bars on the head.

DISTRIBUTION AND HABITAT: Africa, south of the Sahara to Angola and Damaraland; in many species and subspecies. They live in swamps, bogs, marshland, and other wet areas; in small flocks or family parties. During the breeding season in pairs.

CAPTIVITY: Small, terrestrial birds, with short tails and strong, long legs. They have a whirring flight. The aviary floor can best be covered with high

Ortygospiza atricollis.

Padda oryzivora.

171

grasses, patches of granulated peat moss, and such. They are far from strong, and extra care must therefore be taken: feet must be kept clean. They must have small seeds that are offered on the ground, and during the breeding season, live food (ant pupae, cut-up mealworms, green flies, etc.) must be available on a daily basis. The female lays four to six eggs in a little nest near the ground in a grass tussock. Incubation about 11 days. The young leave the nest after approximately two weeks, but will still be fed by both parents for quite some time. These birds often fly perpendicularly, so it is necessary to attach some soft material against the inside of the cage's roof.

FOOD: See BENGALESE.

Genus *Padda* (Java Sparrows)

Java Sparrow   *Padda oryzivora*

DESCRIPTION: Pale blue-gray; head black with white cheek patches. Black tail. Eyes brown, beak pink, legs flesh-colored. The female is somewhat smaller; narrower crown and a more regularly tapered bill. The base of the male's bill is more swollen and a brighter red. Length: six inches (14 cm.).

DISTRIBUTION AND HABITAT: Java, Bali, and various neighboring islands (Indonesia); introduced into Sri Lanka, southern Burma, Zanzibar, St. Helena, among other places.

CAPTIVITY: Currently a very popular aviary bird in Europe. Several mutations have already been developed. The white, pied, and brown mutations have gained quite a following, and in 1973 I came across a blackheaded Java Sparrow in Belgium. These birds are ideal cage (large) and aviary inhabitants. They prefer using half-open nest boxes 12″ × 10″ × 10″; 30 × 25 × 25 cm.) or beechwood blocks (the entrance hole should have a diameter of two inches; 5 cm.). If nothing is done to prevent it, the birds will breed throughout the year, which, of course, could lead to egg-binding problems. Limit the breeding period from May through July and no more than four clutches per season. The incubation period is 12-15 days. If the aviary is fairly peaceful, with only a few fellow inhabitants, success is guaranteed. To discourage fighting, do not hang the breeding boxes close together. Never house two pairs in one cage or aviary; always keep three or more pairs. The white mutation is by far the easiest to breed. The male has a nice bell-like song.

The species *Padda fuscata* or Timor Finch, from Timor, Saman and the Sunda Islands, has rarely been imported in the USA; it seems very rare in the wild. The bird is mainly chocolate-brown, with a white belly and undertail coverts; head and throat are black; cheeks white.

FOOD: Although the birds raise their young without animal protein, it is advisable to present the Bengalese's menu.

Genus *Poephila* (Grass Finches)

Black-throated Finch   *Poephila cincta*

DESCRIPTION: Silverish-gray head; black throat and lores. Fawn back, brownish on the wings. Black tail and bar over the rump. White uppertail coverts. Breast and underparts cinnamon; white under the tail. Black patch on the sides. Eyes dark brown, beak dark gray, legs flesh-colored. Length: four inches (10 cm.).

DISTRIBUTION AND HABITAT: Cape York to South Queensland and the New South Wales border (Australia), in three subspecies. They live in forest, woodland, and scrubby country; near watercourses, and open plains. Near the coast in small flocks.

CAPTIVITY: Sociable, but sometimes aggressive in captivity. They need space; hence a large, well-planted aviary is necessary. More pairs together (that means at least three pairs, never only two) stimulate social behavior and nest building. They build a bottle-like nest of grass, feathers, and plant fibers, with an entrance tunnel, but prefer using a nest box or the old nests of other birds. They like to have a choice, so supply plenty of housing facilities. The female lays five to nine eggs; both sexes incubate for approximately 13 days. The young leave the nest after three weeks and are fed by both parents. In addition to small ripe and half-ripe seeds, insects are essential during the breeding season.

FOOD: See ZEBRA FINCH.

OTHER NAME: Parson Finch.

Long-tailed Finch   *Poephila acuticauda*

DESCRIPTION: Like *P. cincta*. The black tail has two long central feathers like fine needles. Eyes dark brown, beak yellow, legs red. The female has slightly smaller markings; her call is lower in pitch and softer. Length: seven inches (18 cm.).

DISTRIBUTION AND HABITAT: Northern and northwestern Australia; in two subspecies; high in eucalyptus trees and open forests; rarely in open grassland and scrub country. Always near watercourses.

CAPTIVITY: Extremely sociable in the wild, but sometimes troublesome in an aviary. Can best be kept with larger birds in a well-planted aviary. They must be housed indoors during fall and winter. The female lays five or six eggs; the sexes alternate the incubating for 13 days. Give the birds as many different nest boxes as possible; they must be positioned high behind natural cover and far apart. They will construct roosting nests as well, so be sure to provide enough building materials. Sometimes different pairs will sleep together in

The Parson Finch *(Poephila cincta [Gould])* is also known as the black-throated Finch.

Poephila acuticauda (Gould).

174

those nests. For more details see *P. cincta* and the other Australian Grassfinches.

FOOD: See ZEBRA FINCH.

Masked Finch   *Poephila personata*

DESCRIPTION: Chestnut, darker on the wings; rosy-brown cheeks, neck, and underside; white upper- and under-tail coverts. Black band across the lower back to the sides. Eyes dark brown, beak pale yellow, legs light brownish-pink. The black mask of the female is smaller. Length: five inches (12 cm.).

DISTRIBUTION AND HABITAT: Northern Australia. The subspecies *Poephila p. leucotis* or White-eared Grass Finch, with some white under the eye, is confined to the east coast of the Gulf on Cape York; two subspecies. The birds live on timbered, scrubland and grassy plains, near water courses. Due to its constant search for water, also in gardens and parks; in sometimes large groups, composed of pairs (their pair bond lasts throughout the breeding season).

CAPTIVITY: Excellent, sociable, but noisy birds, which need a large, well-planted aviary. They live mainly on the ground in search for food, but spend their mating season high between the branches of dead scrub and trees. Their nest is bulky, close to the ground, and constructed from grass, small feathers, plant fibers, and wool. In the nest-sites pieces of charcoal are incorporated (for hygroscopic reasons). The female lays four to six eggs; both sexes incubate for 13 days. For more details see other *Poephila*-species.

FOOD: See ZEBRA FINCH.

Genus *Pytilias* (Pytilias)

Red-winged Pytilia   *Pytilia phoenicoptera*

DESCRIPTION: Ashy-gray above. The light gray head has dark gray streaks. Rump, wings, and upper tail-coverts are crimson; central tail feathers crimson also; rest of the tail blackish. Underside gray with white bars. The female is browner and has many more markings on belly and breast than the male. Eyes brown, beak black, legs light red-brown. Length: five inches (12 cm.).

DISTRIBUTION AND HABITAT: From western to eastern Africa; in three subspecies. Especially in bushes and tall grass, sometimes close to small villages. They live on insects and seeds.

CAPTIVITY: These birds are suitable for cages and aviaries, although the temperature must not fall below 68° F (20° C). Therefore, a pair can best be kept in an indoor, well-planted aviary with other finches. During the breeding season, they protect their nest very aggressively. The small, untidy nest is built free in a bush or in a box, from grass, hay, small feathers, etc. Feathers are usually used for lining the inside of the nest. A pair breeds well, although they do not like to be disturbed. The male sings a soft, pleasant song practically all day long. In the breeding season, the cock dances round the female with a beautiful raised tail and bowing head. The hen lays three or four eggs; incubation time, 12 days. About 20 days later, the young leave the nest. After approximately eight weeks, they will have their first moult. In the wild this species serves as brood host to the Congo Whydah (*Vidua orientalis interjecta*). The subspecies *Pytilia p. lineata* or Red-billed Aurora Finch, has a red beak. The Yellow-winged or Red-faced Pytilia (*Pytilia hypogrammica*) serves as brood host to the Togo Whydah (*Vidua orientalis togoensis*) and lives in a small strip of land along the Atlantic Ocean from Sierra Leone to Cameroon. The bird looks very similar to the Orange-winged Pytilia, is seldom available but is easy to breed in a well-planted garden aviary, at a temperature of about 68° F (20° C) and up. During the fall and winter all Pytilias must be housed indoors at room temperature.

FOOD: See MELBA FINCH.

OTHER NAMES: Crimson-winged Waxbill, Aurora Finch.

Melba Finch *Pytilia melba*

DESCRIPTION: Throat, chin, and forehead scarlet; rest of head gray. Wings and back olive-green; tail blackish. Chest olive. Underside gray with white streaks and spots. Eyes are brown, beak scarlet, legs brown. The female is duller, lacks all crimson, and has a gray head. Length: five inches (12 cm.).

DISTRIBUTION AND HABITAT: Africa, south of the Sahara; in thorny thickets. The birds live on seeds and, during the breeding season, on insects. This species serves as brood host to the Paradise Whydah (*Vidua paradisea*).

CAPTIVITY: After acclimatization at a temperature of about 77° F (25° C), and no green foods for at least three weeks, the birds can be housed in an indoor, well-planted, and sunny aviary. An outside aviary is suitable only during the hot summer months. This species is usually quite aggressive towards other birds, so it is advisable to keep only one pair in a community aviary. The male has a soft, sweet song. These finches spend a lot of time on the ground looking for small insects, spiders, seeds and such. They build a little domed nest in a small bush; seldom do they use a commercial wooden nest box. The female lays three or four eggs; both partners incubate the clutch for about 12 days and rear the youngsters. However, quite often after two or three days the parents throw their young out of the nest, even when the food is right. The only way to prevent this is to give a rich variety of insects and small seeds, and hope for the best.

The seldom imported Orange-winged Pytilia (*Pytilia afra*) serves as

Pytilia melba.

Poephila personata.

177

Spermestes (Lonchura) nana.

Rufous-backed Mannikin *(Spermestes bicolor).*

brood host for the Broad-tailed Whydah (*Vidua orientalis*), lives in East Africa and surrounding areas, and has an interesting display during the breeding season. In order to impress his partner, the male jumps over her; a kind of leap-frog play, which can also be seen with Gouldian Finches. Females often suffer from egg binding. I feel it necessary to house this species indoors at room temperature; breeding successes are then very well possible.

FOOD: a good commercial seed mix, with a rich variety of millets; also canary grass seed, spray millet, grass and weed seeds. Greens (lettuce, chickweed, dandelion) are essential, although not all birds like it. Throughout the year a variety of insects are necessary: cut-up mealworms, white worms, small maggots, ant pupae, tubifex, spiders, etc. During the breeding season: white bread, soaked in milk or water, egg food, rearing food for finches, cuttle bone, vitamins and minerals.

OTHER NAME: Crimson-faced Waxbill.

Genus *Spermestes* (Mannikins)

Madagascar Mannikin   *Spermestes [Lonchura* or *Lepidopygia] nana*

DESCRIPTION: Olive brown; black lores, throat, and chin; gray underparts mixed with brown on the belly. Sexes are alike. Eyes brown, upper mandible black, lower mandible gray-blue, legs horn-colored. Length: four inches (9 cm.).

DISTRIBUTION AND HABITAT: Madagascar, in groups of about 40 birds. Bush country, grassland and farmland, often near villages.

CAPTIVITY: These birds—rare in the United States—are easy to breed in a well-planted aviary. The male dances before its hen and sings a soft, pretty song consisting of four phrases, repeated three or four times. They also like to chase each other as well as other birds, especially when the latter come too close to their nest. For this reason, I prefer to keep them in a small separate aviary, instead of in a community one, although they are not aggressive birds. Their nest is usually built in thick bushes. They also accept nest boxes. The female lays three or four, sometimes up to seven, white eggs. Incubation time, 12 days. After 21 days, the young leave the nest, but will be cared for by both parents for another 12-14 days, before they become independent. They do not attain full adult plumage for two years. During the breeding season, live insects and germinated seeds are essential.

FOOD: See BENGALESE.

OTHER NAMES: Nana, Bib Finch and African Parson Finch.

Black and White Mannikin   *Spermestes [Lonchura] bicolor*

DESCRIPTION: Black, glossy with bronze green; lower breast and the remaining underparts white; flanks with white scalloping. The sexes are alike. Eyes brown, beak dark gray, legs black. Length: four inches (10 cm.).

DISTRIBUTION AND HABITAT: For the nominate race *bicolor*: West Africa (lacks the stripes on wings and rump). The subspecies *nigriceps* or Rufous-backed Mannikin, is from the east coast of Africa; the bird has a brown back. *L. b. poensis* or Fernando Po Mannikin, has many white spots on the wings and comes, obviously, from Fernando Po; while *stigmatophora* has a black-brown back. The *L. b. woltersi*, which lives south of Zaire, has an extremely brown back. In the south, *rufodorsalis* occurs, with a fox-brown back and white underparts. The smallest subspecies is *minor*, from the north of Africa. All birds live in forests and in secondary growth.

CAPTIVITY: The cock has a soft song. They are reputed to be fairly good breeders and not quarrelsome, except toward their own kind, when housed in a well-planted aviary together with other small finches. The usual commercial nesting boxes are necessary. The building materials that can be offered are grass, hay, wool, and coconut fibers. The female lays three or four eggs, which are incubated by both partners for about 13 days. The young leave the nest when they are about two weeks old.

FOOD: See BENGALESE.

OTHER NAMES: Fernando Po Mannikin or Black-breasted Mannikin.

Bronze-winged Mannikin   *Spermestes [Lonchura] cucullatus*

DESCRIPTION: Head, neck, and throat black; upperparts dark brown. Uppertail-coverts and sides with dark brown stripes; underside buff; scapulars metallic green. Eyes brown, beak gray (the upper mandible is darker), legs dark gray. The beak of the female is often more regularly tapered than the male's. Length: four inches (9 cm.).

DISTRIBUTION AND HABITAT: Africa, south of the Sahara, to Angola and Zimbabwe; also the islands of Pemba, Zanzibar, Mafia, Comoro Islands, and certain islands in the Gulf of Guinea; in open country, farmland, and near villages.

CAPTIVITY: These are very friendly, lively little birds, although they can be and usually are aggressive in the breeding season, even attacking larger birds. The male dances and sings a barely audible purring call during the spring and summer. They don't breed easily, however. To increase chances of breeding success, a well-planted, quietly situated outdoor aviary, housing this species only, should be provided. Commercial nest boxes, and a wide variety of building materials (dry grass, hay, wool, hemp, moss, etc.) are necessary. The

Spermestes bicolor nigriceps.

Lonchura (Spermestes) cucullatus.

Spermestes fringilloides.

four to six eggs will hatch in 12-13 days; both sexes share the task of rearing their young. After 18 days the young leave the nest, but both parents continue to feed them for another 14 days. After this time, however, they must be separated from their parents, to prevent fighting.

FOOD: See BENGALESE.

OTHER NAME: Hooded Finch.

Magpie Mannikin *Spermestes [Lonchura] fringilloides*

DESCRIPTION: Head, flanks, rump, upper tail-coverts and tail glossy black. Wings dusky, underparts off-white. The feathers of the mantle are brown. Typical lancet-shaped tail. Eyes brown, upper mandible dark blue-gray, lower mandible light blue-gray, legs dark gray. The sexes are alike. Length: five inches (12 cm.).

DISTRIBUTION AND HABITAT: Africa, from Senegal to Somalia, and south to Natal; in jungle, grassland and cultivated areas; in small groups.

CAPTIVITY: These birds can be quite aggressive during the breeding season, especially toward small waxbills. Their care and breeding cycle parallels that of the BENGALESE. They must be brought indoors into a lightly heated area for the winter months, and must have access to insects during the breeding period.

FOOD: See BENGALESE.

Genus *Stizoptera* (Double-bar Finches)

Bicheno's Finch *Stizoptera [Poephila] bichenovii*

DESCRIPTION: Light brown, with fine bars. Black wings with white dots. Tail black; rump white. Forehead dark brown; two black bands across breast and neck. Throat, face, and underparts white, with a buff sheen. Eyes dark brown, beak gray, legs dark gray-brown. The female is duller. This species is the smallest of all Australian grass finches. Length: three to four inches (eight to ten cm.).

DISTRIBUTION AND HABITAT: Eastern New South Wales, Queensland (except the southwestern parts), northern areas of Northern Territory, and northwestern Western Australia; in two subspecies. In long grass and scrub (pandanus), near water; also in cane fields, parks and gardens.

CAPTIVITY: An extremely friendly and peaceful aviary bird that must be housed indoors during fall and winter. They are often found on the ground, and it is advisable to have a leaf-mold compost heap in one of the corners. This heap should give the birds the opportunity to look for insects, satisfying their urge for scratching. This species builds its own little nests from grass and feathers, in thick shrubbery, or uses a nesting box. The female lays four or five eggs, which are incubated for 14 days by both sexes. During the night, both partners sit on the nest. In addition to insects, standard seed mixtures are needed. They drink by sucking, as do Zebra Finches. The subspecies with the black rump is scientifically named *Stizoptera bichenovii annulosa* and lives in Northern Territory and the northwestern parts of Australia. In the wild both species cross-breed.

FOOD: See ZEBRA FINCH and other Australian Grass Finches.

OTHER NAMES: Double-barred Finch, Owl-faced Finch, Owl Finch.

Genus *Taeniopygia* (Zebra Finches)
Zebra Finch   *Taeniopygia [Poephila] guttata*

DESCRIPTION: Gray-blue head and neck; drab gray-brown back; dark gray-brown wings; blue-gray chest with black wavy markings; the lower parts of the chest are black; sides orange-red with round white spots; belly beige-white; tail black with white diagonal bands; white "moustache"; orange-red ear spots; under the eye a black band marking the front edge of the ear spot. Eyes red, beak deep red, legs yellow-brown. The female is gray above with a gray, sometimes almost white, ear spot. Throat, neck, chest, and sides gray. Length: four inches (10 cm.).

DISTRIBUTION AND HABITAT: Australia, except the coastal areas of New South Wales and Victoria. A subspecies is found in Timor.

In the wild the Zebra Finch is one of the most common of all so-called Australian grass finches. In northern Australia, it is found mostly in little trees and bushes in overgrown grassland as well as on open savannas. In central Australia, it is often found in rugged, coarse plants (called mulga by the natives) which require little water. It also is found in areas where spinifex, a coarse grass with twisted blades, grows. Here the Zebra Finch looks for young trees and shrubs in which to conceal itself or build a nest.

Since the earliest colonization, the number of Zebra Finches in these dry areas has sharply increased due to the construction of sewage systems, water tanks and watering places for livestock. In the thickly populated areas of eastern, southeastern and southwestern Australia, these birds are a familiar signt around houses, parks, gardens, orchards, and meadows with wooded groves. Zebra Finches in the wild are not shy, but they never become as trusting and familiar as, for example, the Sydney Waxbill (*Aegintha temporalis*) or Bicheno Finch (*Poephila bichenovii*), refusing to sit on a window-sill or balcony.

Areas lacking water also lack Zebra Finches, which accounts for the fact that the bird is seen so rarely in northern and central Australia. It stays mostly on the ground, hopping about on both feet at the same time, much like the House Sparrow (*Passer domesticus*).

The Zebra Finch's diet consists primarily of ripe and half-ripe grass seeds,

183

Stizoptera bichenovii.

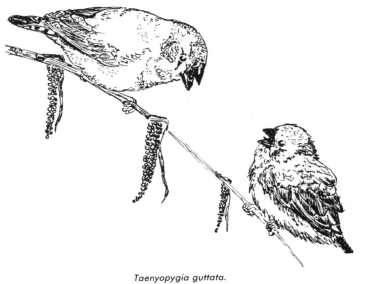

Taenyopygia guttata.

184

although insects also are accepted. The finches often can be seen chasing termites and other small insects that move through the air; among scattered leaves, they seize upon insects. They also can be observed springing up from the ground into the air to snatch windborne grass seeds.

Zebra Finches (like all the other grass finches) drink like pigeons, sucking up the water rather than scooping it the way chickens do. In the wild, I have seen Zebra Finches drinking in the company of other birds, such as Diamond Doves (*Geopelia cuneata*), Cockatiels (*Nymphicus hollandicus*), and Budgerigars (Parakeets) (*Melopsittacus undulatus*).

Zebra Finches in captivity are known for their trumpeting, but this well-known call is not typical of wild birds. Only the males sing at great length and it probably can be thought of as an expression of contentment. Singing in the natural state can most often be heard when the little birds are alone, and it most frequently occurs after mating.

Generally, nests can be found in low thorny bushes or young trees, as well as in wooded groves that stand partly in water. Less common are nests built on the ground in clumps of grass, in tree or rabbit holes. Other unusual nesting places include termite hills, the substructure of nests belonging to birds of prey, nests taken away from other grass finches, swallow nests; under roofs, in gutters, in sheds.

The nest is constructed of rough grass, upholstered inside with soft grass and bits of fruit fuzz. The actual egg cup is prepared with feathers, rabbit fur, and sheep wool. In places where it is difficult to find grass, the nest exterior is made of fine little twigs and roots. Nests built in such places can be described as bottle-shaped, with an entrance on the side. If the nest happens to be built in a hollow, the birds do not bother to build their own roof at all.

Outside the breeding season, nests are frequently built for playing and sleeping, but these nests usually are missing the tunnel-like entrance. Old brood nests also are used as sleeping places.

The future nursery is built by both parents, but usually the male collects and brings in the building materials while the female works them into the nest structure. Perhaps both birds toil at building a nest quickly so it can be completed by the time the rains come. Under normal conditions, Zebra Finches take their time, and it can take as long as two weeks to get the "cradle" ready.

A word of caution: Zebra Finches are enthusiastic builders that will continue building nests until they run out of material. Therefore, it is advisable to limit construction supplies to only as much as is necessary for one round of breeding; if they are given too much, they will continue to build. This keeps them so busy that they often do not get on with the business of egg-laying!

The Zebra Finch advances rapidly in breeding condition after rainfall at any time of the year, but especially in May. The breeding season occurs at different times in different parts of Australia because, to a great extent, successful breeding hinges on rainfall. In central Australia, nest building begins with the first rainfall, independent of the time of year. As we all know, where rain falls, there usually are plants, and where there are plants, there is food. Because it is possible that the rains will be of short duration, the birds begin to build their nests as quickly as possible to breed and raise at least one brood. (In areas of greater rainfall, the "Australian Sparrow" breeds from October to April.)

Next to the importance of rain, successful breeding depends on the temperature. This can be observed in southwestern Australia, where the winters bring too much rain, so nesting takes place in autumn and spring. In summer, there is no rain, and in winter, it is too cold. However, if rain should happen to fall in summer, the birds begin to breed immediately.

In other places, such as eastern Australia, Zebra Finches breed the entire year—with the exception of June, July, November and December.

Many breeders make the common mistake of starting breeding too early. Zebra Finches should be restrained; otherwise, in the dead of winter, they might be setting on eggs in their nests and expecting babies during the most barren of seasons. Early breeding can cause the females to lose much of their strength, which adversely affects future broods. Young birds from early matings generally are not too strong, as become apparent when you wish to breed them after eight months.

Begin breeding at the end of March or the beginning of April with pairs that have been separated during the winter months. You can anticipate three to four broods that, with good care, should be strikingly pure.

As a rule, displays, or so-called mating dances, take place in small dead trees or bushes, since the leaves of live vegetation hinder the birds in their motions. They also are known to mate on the ground or on rocks.

During display, the male Zebra Finch, unlike almost all other Australian grass finches, does not hold a blade of grass or straw, or a feather in his beak. The male and female introduce themselves by jumping up and down between two branches while rubbing their beaks over and over again, pointing their tails at each other. When the female stops, the male moves along the branch toward her in a rhythmic, turning dance, rotating his feet and body with each jump. The male's white belly feathers are expanded; his crown feathers lie flat; the feathers on the back of the head and cheeks stand upright, accenting the black and white portion of the head and the chestnut-brown cheeks. As he approaches, his appearance and song impress the female, and she begins to move her tail up and down, joining him in fluttering. The mating takes place.

Zebra Finches in captivity put on very much the same display. The dance and the mating can occur several times in succession. After the mating, the male places himself in a horizontal position and makes an up and down vibrating motion with his tail, corresponding with the behavior of the female. This has been referred to as "pseudo-female behavior."

Even though birds raised in captivity do not seem to unduly concern themselves about remaining with one mate, it is presumed by ornithologists that Zebra Finches in the wild pair for a lifetime. After mating, the pair lives together the entire year and even stays together when they join huge flocks. One would expect this during the breeding season, but Zebra Finches maintain their relationships beyond the breeding season.

Clutches can range from three to eight eggs, but generally there are four, five or six. They are a pale blue-white, measuring about a half-inch in size.

Brooding—by both parents—begins after the fourth or fifth egg is laid. The male and female relieve each other after periods of two or three hours. They do not change places at the nest but at a short distance away; this is probably done to lead possible enemies away from the actual nest. It is interesting to note that when the male returns to the nest, he often will have a bit of grass, down or feathers in his beak; to the best of my knowledge, the female never does this. Apparently, as a way of "relaxing," the male works the bit he brings into the nest wall. After twilight, both partners go into the nest, but with the first light of day, the male leaves.

The young hatch in 12 to 16 days. It is not possible to give the exact length of the brooding time, because it depends on numerous factors such as the intensity of brooding and the state of the weather.

Baby Zebra Finches just out of the egg are flesh-colored and almost totally bare. By the time they are three days old, their skin is noticeably darker, and within a week it is black. Their beaks also are quite light at the outset; these too become black after about 12 days, turning a fully-colored red after 10 weeks (although remaining a bit lighter than that of the adult bird).

The offspring are blind at hatching, but after eight to ten days they open their eyes; at about the same time, their first feathers appear. For the first two or three days, the babies are totally mute as well, but after that, soft "tearing" sounds can be heard. With each passing day, this "begging call" becomes louder, shriller and more intense.

Food, brought in by both parents, consists of half-ripe seeds from grasses and other plants, along with soft, non-brittle insects. After about three weeks, depending upon the availability of food, the weather and other factors, the offspring fly out of the nest. In the beginning, the parents lead them back to the nest to sleep in the evening. It also has been observed that during the day the parents will entice the young into the nest to make sure they get something to eat, a phenomenon rarely seen among Zebra Finches raised in captivity.

Moulting begins after two months and lasts from one month to six weeks. The family relationship is maintained for some time, the offspring returning to the parental home to sleep. When the parents begin to build a new nest for a new clutch of eggs, however, the time has come for the young ones to take off on their own, though some of them return regularly to the old nest (which is no longer used as a breeding place).

Zebra Finches live in a very social life. In the wild, outside of the breeding season, they can be seen in large flocks of 40 to more than 100 birds. When weather conditions and food supply are good, the birds are content to remain in the same place for the entire year, building their nests and disappearing into them with their partners each evening.

In areas where the probability of drought is great, such as central and northern Australia, Zebra Finches move in search of water. At such times, flocks of hundreds and even thousands can be seen.

In the breeding season, they stay near one another—although never in great numbers—in colonies of five to thirty pairs. For the most part, each pair has its own tree or bush, but where suitable growth is sparse, two or three nests can be found in one tree or sturdy bush.

It has been contended by Prof. Dr. Karl Immelmann that members of such a colony have a strong mutual contact with one another, apparently recognizing one another's calls. Neighbors can come to one another's nests, but strangers beware.

Several times a day, the whole colony goes off to a watering hole to drink, bathe, preen, etc. Sometimes the urge to socialize is so strong that they all come to the same spot to sing. This usually occurs in the middle of the colony, and the whole population joins in, usually during the late afternoon. For more details regarding the studies of behavior of Zebra Finches, conducted by Immelmann and the author of this book, see the book *Zebra Finches* by Hans-Jürgen Martin (Barron's, Woodbury, New York, 1985).

CAPTIVITY: Zebra Finches are particularly well-suited for anyone who is just beginning to keep birds. Keeping a single pair in a large cage for their song or color—or keeping several pairs for breeding—is not a difficult task and there isn't any magic connected with it.

Zebra Finches not only demand little in the way of care, but have a bright and vigorous song and are easy to breed. And, without a doubt, Zebra Finches also win the hearts of many experienced bird breeders because they offer endless opportunities to achieve fascinating color varieties through breeding experimentation. Zebra Finches are prolific breeders in outdoor aviaries, but only three or four broods per season are recommended. Remove all nesting materials (grass, plant fibers, feathers, moss, wool), as soon as the nest is completed, to prevent further construction. The free nest is bottle-shaped, with an entrance tunnel. They like to use all types of nest boxes and such. The female lays four or five eggs, which are incubated by both sexes for about 13-16 days. The young leave the nest after 20-22 days.

FOOD: See BENGALESE, and text above.

OTHER NAMES: Zebrafinch and Chestnut-eared Finch.

Genus *Uraeginthus* (Blue Waxbills and Grenadiers)

Angola Cordon Bleu   *Uraeginthus angolensis*

DESCRIPTION: Almost identical to the Red-cheeked Cordon Bleu (*U.*

188

bengalus); this species lacks the crimson-red ear patches. Tail and rump blue; upper parts mouse brown, breast and flanks sky blue. Lower breast and abdomen whitish-brown. Eyes brown, beak reddish-gray, with a black tip, legs light brown. The females are somewhat paler in coloration and have creamy underparts, but are difficult to distinguish from other female Cordon Bleus, although their beaks are usually a much brighter pink. Length: five inches (12 cm.).

DISTRIBUTION AND HABITAT: From Zaire to Tanzania and south to Transvaal (South Africa); introduced into Zanzibar and São Thomé; in scrub country and cultivated areas (gardens, parks) in sometimes large flocks. Their oven-shaped nests are built of fine grasses and small feathers.

CAPTIVITY: Excellent for large aviaries and cages, where they brood in half-open nest boxes. The female lays three or four eggs. For further details see RED-CHEEKED CORDON BLEU. This species is usually very friendly toward other small African finches, although they are sometimes antagonistic toward the Red-cheeked Cordon Bleu. Although sudden temperature changes can chill the birds, they resist lower temperatures far better than *U. bengalus*. During fall and winter the species belongs indoors, however (minimal 65° F; 18° C).

FOOD: Similar to that of the RED-CHEEKED CORDON BLEU.

OTHER NAME: Blue-breasted Waxbill.

Blue-capped Cordon Bleu   *Uraeginthus cyanocephalus*

DESCRIPTION: Very similar to the Angola Cordon Bleu (*U. angolensis*), but with a splendidly blue-colored head and brown upperparts. Tail blue. Eyes reddish-brown, beak pink or crimson-red with a black tip, legs light brown. Females lack the blue head, although quite often some blue on the forehead may be seen. Length: five inches (13 cm.).

DISTRIBUTION AND HABITAT: East Africa, from Ethiopia to Tanzania, in arid grass and thornbush country. The birds search primarily for grass and weed seeds, small insects and spiders. Their nests are mostly constructed in thorny bushes, often close to wasps' nests.

CAPTIVITY: Is somewhat shyer than the Angola Cordon Bleu. If acclimatized properly this species breeds regularly in a large, well-planted aviary. For more detailed information see ANGOLA CORDON BLEU.

FOOD: See RED-CHEEKED CORDON BLEU.

OTHER NAMES: Blue-headed Cordon Bleu and Blue-headed Waxbill.

Uraeginthus angolensis.

The Cordon Bleu *(Uraeginthus bengalus)* is a popular, easily raised and propogated finch species in aviculture. This bird is sexually dimorphic with the cock exhibiting the typical chestnut cheek patch. A hen is shown here.

Photo by author

Uraeginthus cyanocephalus.

Purple Grenadier   *Uraeginthus ianthinogaster*

DESCRIPTION: Head, neck and upperparts chestnut. Breast blue with red and reddish-brown spots. Eye-ring red with a sky-blue patch above and below the eye. Wings dark brown, tail black, rump blue. Chin and throat reddish-brown; underside violet. Eyes dark brown, beak red, legs anthracite-colored. The female doesn't have any blue coloration, except for the rump; the area around the eyes is white. The breast often has some brown-yellowish and whitish specks. Young birds still have a black beak, and miss all the blue. Length: six inches (14 cm.).

DISTRIBUTION AND HABITAT: East Africa, especially from Ethiopia east to Somalia, Kenya and southern Tanzania, in three subspecies. They live in arid open grassland and thornbush country, where they search primarily in pairs for termites, grass and weed seeds. They are almost completely insectivorous during the breeding season. This species is parasitized by the Fischer's Whydah (*Vidua fischeri*).

CAPTIVITY: First bred by Mr. E.J. Boosey (England, 1957); breeding successes, however, remain rare. A free nest is often fragile, round with a side entrance. The birds prefer half-open or enclosed nest boxes; both sexes build. Soft materials, like grass, wool and feathers, are important. The female lays three to five eggs. Incubation period: 13-14 days. Both sexes incubate, the female primarily during the night. The young leave the nest when 20-22 days old; after another two weeks they are independent. For more details see VIOLET-EARED WAXBILL (*U. granatina*). Experience has taught me that a pair can be quite aggressive in a mixed collection. A large aviary, with thick planting, is therefore advisable. Breeding pairs, however, can best be housed in a separate facility where they settle quickly and become surprisingly trustful toward the keeper; they don't even mind an occasional peek in their nest. Their song sounds like that of the Violet-eared Waxbill but is chirpier and more canary-like.

FOOD: Normal seed mix for small finches. During the breeding season various insects (ant pupae, white worms, maggots, and—their favorites—small, cut-up mealworms) are absolutely essential, as are water- or milk-soaked white bread, finch rearing food, sprouted seeds and millet spray.

OTHER NAME: Purple-bellied Waxbill.

Red-cheeked Cordon Bleu   *Uraeginthus bengalus*

DESCRIPTION: Underside brownish-gray; cheeks, throat, sides, breast and uppertail coverts sky blue; tail duller blue. Crimson ear patches. Abdomen whitish-brown. Eyes brown, beak pink-reddish with an ashy-black tip, legs light horn colored. The female is somewhat paler and lacks the red ear patches. The red ear patches in young males appear when the birds are approximately 10 weeks old. Length: five inches (12 cm.).

DISTRIBUTION AND HABITAT: From Senegal to Ethiopia and south through eastern Africa to Katanga and Zambia; in open country, savanna, woodland, semi-arid thornscrub and cultivated areas. In the wild, nests are often found in the immediate vicinity of hornets' and wasps' nests (protection against nest predators!). The subspecies *U. b. schoanus,* from Ethiopia, distinguishes itself through a longer tail and darker colors, but is rarely seen in aviculture.

CAPTIVITY: Acclimatization must be realized with the greatest of care. The first few weeks after arrival the birds must be housed in a box cage or indoor aviary at a minimal temperature of 75° F (23° C). This species can't be kept in housing facilities where the temperature is below 65° F (18° C). Provide new arrivals with small millets, oranges, and bananas. We can sprinkle universal or finch-rearing food over the fruits. This way the birds get accustomed to these new foods. Acclimatized birds are far from fragile and may be kept in outdoor aviaries during the late spring and summer months, together with other small finches. This species prefers to breed in garden aviaries with thick plantings and a variety of box nests and half-open nest boxes. I have known birds that lived for more than 10 years in captivity! Although the birds occupy various types of nest boxes—provided they are placed high in the aviary—they sometimes build a free nest in a thick bush. Offer long stems of dry grass, moss, wool, coconut fibers, small feathers and the like. The female lays four or five eggs; larger clutches are usually from two females. After 11-13 days the young hatch; after 30-40 days the young males can be distinguished from the females, as the red ear patches become visible.

The song of this species is pleasant and clear. During courtship the male dances in front of the hen with a long blade of grass in his beak. During the day both partners brood alternately, but during the evening and night usually only the female is "on duty." During warm days the parents often cover the eggs with nesting material and leave the clutch to its fate for many hours. Hybrids are possible with Bengalese, St. Helena Waxbill, Blue-breasted Waxbill, and Blue-headed Waxbill. Towards the end of summer, Cordon Bleus are best housed in indoor aviaries or large cages.

FOOD: All kinds of small millets, spray millet, grass and weed seeds, germinated seeds, greens and, during the breeding season, various small insects, spiders, finch-rearing food, soaked white bread, cuttle bone, etc. Without animal protein, however, breeding successes will be rare.

OTHER NAMES: Cordonbleu and Blue-headed Waxbill.

Violet-eared Waxbill *Uraeginthus granatina*

DESCRIPTION: Male primarily chestnut, with deep violet ear patches and forehead; eye-ring red. Rump and uppertail and undertail coverts dark blue; wings brownish-gray. Chin, throat, vent, and tail black. Eyes reddish-brown, beak red, legs brown. The female is duller, with grayish upperparts and yellowish-brown underparts. The throat is whitish. There is no blue on the

192

undertail coverts. Young birds resemble the female, but they still have black beaks; the rump, however, is already blue. Males and females have an exceptionally pleasant and clear song. Their communication calls resemble those of the Red-cheeked Cordon Bleu. Length: five inches (13 cm.).

DISTRIBUTION AND HABITAT: From Angola to Zambia (Africa), in thorn-scrub country and arid areas; in pairs or small flocks, quite often together with *U. angolensis*. The species build their round nests close to the ground (within three feet), in thorny bushes. The bird is parasitized by the Queen Whydah (*Vidua regia*).

CAPTIVITY: This bird is often imported; young birds, however, are difficult to distinguish from *U. angolensis*. The species is very sensitive to disturbances, especially during the breeding season. The best breeding results may be obtained in well-planted, large garden aviaries. The parents must have access to various insects and finch rearing-food. After arrival the birds must be housed for at least four weeks, in a roomy indoor aviary; keep the temperature between 73° and 77° F (23° and 25° C). After the acclimatization period the birds may be placed in garden aviaries, provided the outside temperature is no less than 68° F (20° C).

Although generally friendly, toward members of the same genus they are often hostile and aggressive. A well-planted aviary is the answer if various finch species are kept in the same facility.

I recommend breeding in indoor aviaries, as during the first few days the young don't have much down; temperatures below 77° F (25° C) are often fatal. Supply enough nesting material (wool, grass, moss, coconut fibers, etc.), as well as some small feathers, as the male likes to play with them while sitting on the nest. The female lays four to seven eggs; after approximately 21-24 days the young leave the nest, but will receive the attention of both parents for another two to three weeks. After six to eight weeks the young males are fully colored.

FOOD: Grass and weed seeds, Senegal millet and spray millet. During the breeding season small insects, white bread soaked in water, finch rearing-food and egg food are essential. Provide charcoal and cuttle bone throughout the year. See also RED-CHEEKED CORDON BLEU.

Genus *Zonaeginthus* (Diamond Sparrows)

Diamond Sparrow *Zonaeginthus [Emblema] guttata*

DESCRIPTION: Grayish head, somewhat lighter on the nape, and very light on the neck. Dark gray-brown back and wings; uppertail coverts red, tail black. Lores black; a broad black band crossing the chest. Flank black with white spots; hence the bird's name. Underside and undertail coverts white. Eyes dark brown with a red iris, beak red, legs gray-brown. The female is often somewhat smaller, and occasionally has brownish and smaller lores.

193

Zonaeginthus guttata.

Zonaeginthus bellus.

DISTRIBUTION AND HABITAT: Southern central Queensland, eastern New South Wales to Victoria and South Australia; also on Kangaroo Island. They live in mallee thickets, gardens, parks, grassland, and open woodland. The bird likes to breed in tall grass, near water. They operate in small groups, but during the breeding season live in pairs. Due to serious destruction of their habitat, the numbers of Diamond Sparrows are rapidly decreasing.

CAPTIVITY: This species is not always very active in small cages and aviaries, where they usually become fat and pugnacious. Therefore only suitable for large, well-planted facilities, together with other large finches. They are somewhat aggressive, especially during the breeding season. Never house two pairs in the same cage or aviary. Temperatures below 60° F (15° C) are not well-taken; birds housed in outdoor quarters must be put inside as soon as temperatures start to drop in early fall. Pairs need a good selection of nesting materials; coconut fibers, leaf veins, wool, moss, and soft dry grass (up to 20"—50 cm.—long!), but watch out for long pieces of thread and string, since the parents and young can get tangled in it. A free-standing bullet-shaped nest is usually constructed in a thick bush; the nest often has a long entrance-tunnel. The birds also use various nest boxes. While one of the birds sets on the eggs or is feeding the youngsters, the other partner often makes nest repairs. The hen lays five or six eggs which are incubated by both parents for 12-14 days. The young leave the nest after approximately 30 days; about two weeks later they are already independent and must then be housed in a separate flight, as the male parent often aggressively chases them around. On the other hand, Diamond Sparrows are rather sensitive birds, so they won't always accept their partner; it is therefore advisable to let the birds do the "choosing."

FOOD: Various millets and spray millet, canary grass seed, and ripe and sprouted grass and weed seed. During the year but especially during the breeding season Diamond Sparrows are partly insectivorous; therefore small cut-up mealworms, white worms, and fresh ant pupae are absolutely essential. Without animal protein, chances are that the young will not develop properly.

OTHER NAME: Diamond Finch.

Beautiful Firetail   *Zonaeginthus [Stagonobleura] bellus*

DESCRIPTION: Upperparts brown-gray with brown-black waved design. Wings chocolate-brown with the same waved design. Back, rump, and uppertail coverts red. Tail feathers dark brown with brown-blackish design. Forehead and ear black; chin and throat whitish brown with little brown-blackish waves. Breast, flanks and underside white with waved design. Undertail coverts black. Eyes dark brown with an opal-blue periophthalmic ring, beak red, legs pinkish. The female's ear-stripe is less intense; the belly is lighter. Length: five inches (12 cm.).

DISTRIBUTION AND HABITAT: Australia, from Newcastle to Victoria and the east coast of South Australia, Kangaroo Island and Tasmania; in swamps, grassland, bushes, parks and gardens.

CAPTIVITY: Rarely available. Needs a large, well-planted aviary, without other birds. For more details see DIAMOND SPARROW. The Red-eared Fire Finch (*Z.* or *Stagonopleura occulatus*) looks very similar to the *bellus*, and is extremely rare in aviculture, but requires the same care, management and feed as the Diamond Finch.

Pytilia phoenicoptera.

Appendix

Alphabetical List of Finch Genera

AEGINTHA—Red-browed Finches
AIDEMOSYNE—Cherry Finches
AMADINA—Cut-throat Finches
AMANDAVA—Avadavats
BATHILDA—Star Finches
CHLOEBIA—Gouldian Finches
CLYTOSPIZA—Brown Twin-spots
CRYPTOSPIZA—Crimson- wings
EMBLEMA—Fire-tailed Finches
ERYTHRURA—Parrot Finches
ESTRILDA—Waxbills or Typical Waxbills
EUODICE—Silverbills
EUSCHISTOSPIZA—Dusky Twin-spots
HYPARGOS—Twin-spots
LAGONOSTICTA—Fire Finches
LONCHURA—Mannikins and Munias
MANDINGOA—Green-backed Twin-spots
NEOCHMIA—Crimson Waxbills
NESOCHARIS—Oliveback Finches
NIGRITA—Negro Finches
ODONTOSPIZA—Gray-headed Silverbills
OREOSTRUTHUS—Mountain Finches
ORTYGOSPIZA—Quail Finches
PADDA—Java Sparrows
POEPHILA—Grass Finches
PYTILIA—Pytilias
SPERMESTES—Mannikins
STIZOPTERA—Double-bar Finches
TAENIOPYGIA—Zebra Finches
URAEGINTHUS—Blue Waxbills and Grenadiers
ZONAEGINTHUS—Diamond Sparrows

Above: *Poephila personata*; center: *Poephila cincta*; below: *Poephila acuticauda.*

Specialist Societies

Australian Finch Society of England
478 New Hey Road
Wirral, Merseyside, L49 9DB, ENGLAND

Australian Finch Society of South Africa
116 Woodley Road
Plumestead, 7800, SOUTH AFRICA

Avicultural Society of Australia
56 Harris Road
Elliminyt, Victoria 3249, AUSTRALIA

Avicultural Society of New Zealand
P.O. Box 21-403
Henderson, Auckland 8, NEW ZEALAND

Foreign Bird League
Monk's Cottage, 58 Preston Crowmarsh
Benson, Oxen Ox9 6SL, ENGLAND

International Softbill Society
National Aquarium, Pier 3, 501 East Pratt St.
Baltimore, Maryland 21202, USA

National Bengalese Fanciers' Association
2 Bridge Street
Griffithstown, Gwent, UNITED KINGDOM

National Finch Society
529 Burnside Ave.
East Hartford, Connecticut 06108, USA

Singapore Avicultural Society
c/o Holy Family Church
6 Chapel Road, SINGAPORE 1542

Zebra Finch Society of Canada
R.R. 1
Zephyr, Ontario L0E 1T0, CANADA

Zebra Finch Society of United Kingdom
87 Winn Road, Lee
London SE12 9EY, ENGLAND

Red-eared Firetail Finch *(Zonaeginthus oculatus).*

Plum-capped Finch *(Aidemosyne modesta).*

Bibliography

Magazines

American Cage Bird Magazine (monthly)
1 Glamore Court
Smithtown, NY 11787 (USA)
(Features a bi-monthly directory of bird societies)

Avicultural Bulletin (monthly)
Avicultural Society of America, Inc.
734 North Highland Avenue
Hollywood, CA 90038 (USA)

Bird Talk (monthly)
P.O. Box 3940
San Clemente, CA 92672 (USA)

Bird World (bi-monthly)
P.O. Box 70
North Hollywood, CA 91603 (USA)

Cage and Aviary Birds (weekly published in England)
North American address:
Business Press International (USA)
205 E. 42nd St.
New York, NY 10017

(Young bird keepers under sixteen may like to join the *Junior Bird League*. Full details can be obtained from the J.B.L., c/o *Cage and Aviary Birds*, Prospect House, 9-15 Ewell Road, Cheam, Sutton, Surrey SM3 8BZ, England.)

Finch News
28 Warruga St.
The Gap, Queensland 4061
Australia

The Avicultural Magazine (bi-monthly)
The Avicultural Society of England
Windsor Forest Stud Mill Ride
Ascot, Berkshire, SL5 8LT
England

Watchbird (bi-monthly)
The American Federation of Aviculture
P.O. Box 1568
Redondo Beach, CA 92078 (USA)

Books

Bates, H.J. and Busenbark, R.L. (1978). *Finches and Soft-billed Birds* (T.F.H. Publications Inc., Neptune, NJ).

Boosey, E.J. (1962). *Foreign Bird Keeping* 2nd ed. (Iliffe, London)

Christie, I. (1985). *Birds: A Guide to a Mixed Collection* (Merehurst Press, London).

Gallerstein, G.A., D.V.M. (1984). *Bird Owner's Home Health and Care Handbook* (Howell Book House Inc., New York, NY).

Harman, I. and Vriends, Matthew M. (1978). *All About Finches and Related Seed-eating Birds* (T.F.H. Publications Inc., Neptune, NJ).

Immelmann, K. (1977). *Australian Finches* (Agnus and Robertson, London).

King, B., Woodcock, M. and Dickinson, E.C. (1975). *A Field Guide to the Birds of South-East Asia* (Collins, London).

Martin, Hans-Jurgen (1985). *Zebra Finches* (Barron's, Woodbury, NY).

Restall, L.R. (1975). *Finches and Other Seed-eating Birds* (Faber and Faber, London).

Roberts, A. (1961). *Birds of South Africa* (Revised ed.) (The Trustees of the South African Bird Book Fund, Cape Town).

Robiller, L. (1974). *Cage and Aviary Birds* (Almark Publishing Co., London).

Longtailed Grass Finch cock *(Poephila acuticauda)*.

Rutgers, A. (1977). *The Handbook of Foreign Birds* (Vol. 1, 4th edition) (Blandford Press, Poole).

Rutgers, A. and Norris, K.A. (eds.) (1977). *Encyclopedia of Aviculture* (Vols. 1-3) (Blandford Press, Poole).

Trollope, J. (1983). *The Care and Breeding of Seed-eating Birds* (Blandford Press, Poole).

Vriends, Matthew M. (1985). *Breeding Cage and Aviary Birds* (Howell Book House Inc., New York, NY).

Vriends, Matthew M. (1978). *Handbook of Zebra Finches* (T.F.H. Publications Inc, Neptune, NJ).

Vriends, Matthew M. (1984). *Simon & Schuster's Guide to Pet Birds* (Simon & Schuster, New York, NY).

Yealland, J.J. (1971). *Cage Birds in Colour* (H.F. & G. Witherby Ltd, London).

Green Avadavat cock.